SO-EIR-410

# DATE DUE

Published by:
WorkLife Publishing
4532 E. Grandview Rd., Phoenix, AZ  85032
Phone 602-992-0144, Fax 602-493-9321  www.worklifepublishing.com

Library of Congress Catalog Card Number: 98-061245

Publisher's Cataloging-in-Publication  (Provided by Quality Books, Inc.)
Jordan, Claudia
     Job search secrets : smart strategies to land your dream job /
Claudia Jordan. -- 1st ed.
     p. cm.
     1. Job hunting  I. Title.
     HF5382.7.J67 1998     650.14
                      QBI98-1072

*Printed in the United States of America*
*Cover design by Mark LaLone and Carlos Gonzalez*
*Photograph of author by Steve Thompson*

10   9   8   7   6   5   4   3   2   1

*To my family who has always inspired me
to be the best that I can be.*

# Contents

## Chapter Three: Remarkable Resumes and Cover Letters

## Chapter Four: Networking Know-How

## Chapter Five: Marketing Savvy

## Chapter Six: Ace the Interview

## Chapter Seven:  Gold Medal Techniques

# Chapter One

# Successful Strategies

# Aim for Your Dream Job.

There is no reason to settle for second best when you can have your dream job. Once you decide to go after your dream job, your passion and determination will carry you past the obstacles. The problem is, most people never decide to do it. There is power in deciding. There is power in affirming your decision to be the very best every day. There is power in you, right now. All you have to do to begin is decide—decide to pursue your dream job and excel in your work.

Think of the freedom—and exhilaration—of working in a job you perform well and love! You leap out of bed every morning excited to go to work. Your friends and peers respect you. And because you do something you love, you excel in it and are well paid.

Of course, we know nothing in this world is free. Along with your decision to pursue your dream job comes...dare I say it?...work. The point is that your dream job is attainable, you can have it. But you must do some work to pinpoint just what your dream job is, then how to pursue it in the most successful manner. Perhaps you already know your dream job. Excellent!

What if you don't know what your dream job is? Your dream job is something that you love very much, but may not even recognize it because is it so much a part of your life you think everyone does that or feels that way. Ask yourself these thought provoking questions:

If I was guaranteed $100,000 a year, plus raises, by a trust fund from a distant relative, but I had to work forty hours a week in a job of my choosing, what would I do?

If I received an all expenses gift of going to school full time for two to four years, what would I study?

What was my dream as a kid, teenager, or young adult? What were the experiences or activities I loved the most as a child? (Ask your parents!)

What would I like to have people say about me at my funeral? What would I like my epitaph to say?

What would I like to be known for?

If I could change one thing in the world, what would it be?

What in the world makes me the angriest? (Do something to change it!)

What is my dream job?

Now, I want you to take a few minutes to visualize yourself in your new dream job. Begin as you enter your workplace. What are you wearing? What kind of workplace is it? (Home, warehouse, forest, skyscraper, city streets, small business, Hollywood set, etc.) What hours do you work? As you go to where you perform your work, what kind of people surround you? Are there animals or plants? Now you're at your workplace. What does it look like? Do you have a desk, tools, machines, or computer? What kind of activities do you do all day? What kind of people are your co-workers, customers, consumers, patients, or audience? What is your boss like?

After you have a clear visualization, write it down immediately to reaffirm it. Embellish it with loving details. Put your writing away, and come back to it at a later time. After you read it, decide which things are within your grasp right now, then which things are nice, but not necessary. What does your dream job look like now? In view of your dream job ask yourself these questions:

If I was granted any job I'm capable of right now, what would it be? What progression of jobs will lead to my dream job? What can I do now to start?

*Your Specific Dream*
*+ Burning Desire*
*+ Planned Action*
*= Your Dream Job*

# *Do Not Begin Until You Know What You Want to Do.*

A typical job search goes like this: The job hunter makes up a resume of his past work experience without an objective for his next job. He combs the want ads looking for something that strikes him, "Hey, that looks good, maybe I could do that!" and mails his resume in a scattered manner. He may send his resume to various large corporations hoping the human resource department can find something for him. His friends say, "So-and-so is hiring, you should apply." The job hunter doesn't get very far in this scenario because he has not thought of what he wants to do, what kind of work will he love and be passionate about.

If you know before an interview what you want to do, your chances are far greater of landing your dream job. First of all, you are targeting only the companies that do the work you want, saving you time. Second, you are focused, knowledgeable, and enthusiastic about the work, which rates very high with employers. Even as a career-changer or at an entry level, your background research makes you more knowledgeable than Joe Schmoe randomly mailing his resume and half-heartedly applying for jobs. Nothing can replace pure passion for the work you love.

An easy way to define what you want to do and still allow you flexibility, is to express it in terms of Function/Industry. The function is the actual work you perform and the industry is the field you are interested in. Here are some examples:

Purchasing Agent / Electronics

Health Care Administrator for a hospital.

Sports Events Planner

What industry are you passionate about? What field do you love? What kind of work could you perform in that field using your skills, education, experience, and knowledge?

# *Name Your Top Five Characteristics.*

Your characteristics, or personality traits, will give you clues to what type of work best suites you. And when looking for that type of work, the employer will be looking for specific traits in the perfect candidate. For example, an actor will have strikingly different personality traits than a scientific researcher.

To find out what yours are, ask your friends, co-workers, and family. Which characteristics keep popping up? Here are some examples of characteristics to help you.

| | | | |
|---|---|---|---|
| Accurate | Analytical | Artistic | Committed |
| Competent | Creative | Committed | Determined |
| Energetic | Enthusiastic | Friendly | Goal-oriented |
| Honest | Imaginative | Logical | Motivated |
| Organized | Outgoing | Persuasive | Productive |
| Resourceful | Teamworker | Thorough | Versatile |

Once you have determined some of your characteristics, then think of something you have done at work or in your spare time that illustrates your characteristics. Another way to approach this is to think of an achievement or activity that made you feel on top of the world and identify your characteristics during that time.

Identifying your five best characteristics, and the stories that illustrate them, gives you valuable clues to the type of work that is best for you. Describe the characteristics and stories to several friends, and brainstorm about jobs for that type of personality. Your top personality traits and accompanying stories will come in handy during your job search and interviews.

# Name Your Top Five Skills.

Can you name your top five skills? Can you give examples of how you have best used these skills? Do not even think of going to an interview if you can't answer these questions with confidence. If you can't name your skills then how do you know which jobs to target?

One technique to identify skills is to write out a description of five to seven accomplishments, detailing each step and what the results were. These accomplishments can be drawn from work, volunteer work, hobbies, home skills, or leisure. These stories illustrate your skills. Be sure to write about accomplishments that you really enjoyed to identify the skills you like the best. Perhaps you are an excellent typist but you don't want to be a typist, you want to be a reporter. In that case, other skills would take precedence over the typing skills.

In the appendix of Richard Bolles' *What Color Is Your Parachute?* is an excellent skill assessment chart, laying out skills in clusters with the three main clusters being Interpersonal Skills, Physical

Skills, and Mental Skills. If you are having a difficult time identifying your skills, use these charts. Writing out your accomplishments, then identifying the skills used, affirms (to yourself) your top skills. Prioritize these top five skills. With this information in hand you are better equipped to choose—and land—your dream job.

## *Get Organized.*

Being organized will help you be more productive and find a job faster. Find a space in your home or apartment close to a telephone—a desk, kitchen or dining room table, or corner of your bedroom. Keep your materials nearby.

For supplies you'll need pads of paper, pens, stick-on notes, message notepad, a letter-size file box with manila files, 5 x 7-inch cards, and a box to hold them. You will need good quality stationery and envelopes to print your resume, cover letters, and other correspondence and a supply of thank-you notes. Also highly recommended are business-sized networking cards. (See *Design Networking Cards*, p. 89.)

To keep yourself organized, your tasks prioritized, and your appointments straight, use a personal organizer, either a paper notebook style or electronic. Use a small telephone directory for phone numbers.

A telephone answering machine or voice mail is a must. The greeting your callers hear should be professional, short, and upbeat. One option is to advertise by leaving a message like this: "Hi, this is Bob. Sorry I missed your call, but I'm out pounding the pavement looking for a job as a _____. Please leave a message."

Professional correspondence is a necessity. If you have a computer and a good printer, excellent. If not, find a way to obtain access to one—either through a friend or at a print/copy shop with computers for rent. If you have the means, buying a computer is a good investment and it will probably pay for itself in the long run. It is your personal choice.

Another alternative is to hire a resume service or secretarial service to type letters for you. Look in the phone book under Resume Service or in your local paper near the want ads or under Services. Talk to several. Get quotes, and find out exactly what they will do for you.

A fax machine can be useful. If you don't have one, ask to use your neighbors, or go to your local mailing/shipping store when you need one. Be sure to keep the fax number handy so you'll be prepared when asked for it.

# *Enlist a Mentor.*

Meeting with a friend every week to talk about your job search is beneficial for several reasons. It helps you stay productive since you have to "report" to someone every week, it's uplifting, and you can discuss strategies with your mentor friend.

Try to find someone who is willing to meet with you once a week. A friend or relative with a business background and an open mind is ideal. Your spouse is okay, but it's better to meet with someone outside your home and everyday life. The role your friend plays as mentor is simple: he or she meets with you once a week, listens to your past activities, listens to your plans for the upcoming week, then you both discuss effectiveness, strategies, and ideas. The key here is that your mentor LISTENS. You may have hard days, and it's good to talk about them and get the frustration out of your system. Just don't get hung up on the pitfalls. Your friend can help you out of the doldrums.

It is up to you, the job seeker, to report your past week's activities and share your plans for the following week. (You do have a plan, don't you?) It's your job search, you decide what to do, what action to take. Your mentor is there to listen, provide morale support, and offer ideas. Meeting your mentor every week practically ensures you will be active and have a plan for the next week, because it's embarrassing to meet with your friend with nothing on the agenda. However, if that does happen, then it's time for your friend to motivate you and come up with fresh ideas. Explain to your mentor up front your guidelines for a mentor/job hunter relationship so it goes smoothly.

# Do What You Say You Will Do.

How many people do you know that say one thing and do another, or never follow-through? Do you know someone who does what they say they will do and you can count on it as surely as the sun will come up tomorrow? Which kind of person do you think an employer would like to hire?

During your job search (and after you're hired!), be dependable, punctual, follow-through, display good manners and integrity. These are highly desired traits in the workplace. Your job search is an excellent way to demonstrate character traits and skills you will be using in your next job.

If you write a letter stating you will call to set up a meeting, *then do it.* If you leave a message saying you will call tomorrow at 2 p.m., *then do it.* If you say you'll stop by in the morning to apply for the job, *then do it.* If you say you'll send someone a copy of an article, *then do it.*

If you ask a contact if you may call other people they refer to you, then do it. One woman I met was annoyed that a networking contact did not call any of the three people she referred and vowed not to help that person again.

Being decisive is powerful. Not following through is self-destructive! Demonstrate that you are dependable, punctual, and trustworthy at every opportunity. Actions speak volumes louder than words. Good manners are essential during this time. People respond warmly to gracious people with integrity and good manners.

# *Mind Your Manners.*

A recent article announced that Job Search Etiquette classes are offered by the career counseling departments at some universities. Obviously, there is a need to learn etiquette and it's not limited to young adults. Somehow, in parts of our society, manners have been left along the roadside like a forgotten pair of broken sunglasses. Good manners never go out of style—they are about respect and consideration for others. Practicing proper etiquette during your job search will open doors for you.

Address new people as Mr. (last name) and Ms. (last name), until invited to use their first name. If they have a title such as Dr., use that. Women should be addressed as Ms. __ unless they request differently. Apply this rule to people you meet in person, address in letters, fax, and e-mail—especially your interviewer.

Always write a thank-you note to people who help you, mentioning exactly what they did for you, and mail it within twenty-four hours. (See *Send Thank-You Notes to Everyone Who Helps You*, p. 109.)

Both women and men should offer to shake hands and use a firm handshake.

Conversation is a two-way street, with you talking half the time and the other person talking half the time. Do not interrupt when others are speaking. Make direct eye contact, but don't stare.

Project energy, alertness, and confidence by maintaining good posture. Walk tall, sit tall, keep your back straight. In an interview do not slouch in your chair or perch on the edge like a scared rabbit. Find a comfortable pose and hold your hands in a relaxed, natural position. No hand-wringing, arm-crossing, foot-twitching nervous habits, please. Do not chew gum, suck on mints or candy, or smoke during an interview, even if the interviewer does.

If you are invited to a luncheon interview, your manners should be exemplary. Do not order an alcoholic drink or smoke. (If it is a dinner and the host insists, have one drink.) Order food that is easy to eat and in the mid-price range. Be courteous to the waitress or waiter. Need I mention—use a napkin, don't talk with food in your mouth, chew with your mouth closed, take small bites so you can talk between bites, don't make any smacking or slurping noises, pay more attention to your interviewer than your food, etc.

# *Read Good Job Search Publications.*

Learning more about effective ways to conduct your job search can be very profitable. Sometimes the person who gets the job is the one most knowledgeable about job search—not the one who is best qualified for the job.

Keep in mind to do your reading during your spare time in the evenings or weekends. Reserve prime business hours for your job search. Research should not delay getting started with your search.

Most books and newspapers are free to read at your local library in the reference section.

The *National Business Employment Weekly,* published by *The Wall Street Journal,* contains excellent articles about numerous aspects of the job search. It also compiles the want ads from *The Wall Street Journal.* (See *Get the Most Out of Want Ads,* p.135.) You can visit this site on the Internet at www.nbew.com.

*What Color Is Your Parachute?* by Richard Bolles is updated every year and is especially good for career-changers. Visit the web site at www.washingtonpost.com/wp-adv/classifieds/careerpost/parachute/front.htm.

Another of my books, *JobFinder: How to Find a Better Job Faster* is a practical guide that leads job seekers through the job hunting maze in an easy, step-by-step format. *JobFinder* illustrates how to identify—and land—your ideal work.

Many other books are available at the library or bookstores. *JobFinder* and *What Color Is Your Parachute?* each contain a section about recommended job search books.

# Be Well Dressed and Groomed Whenever You Leave Home.

Imagine stopping for gas and running into the vice president of an important firm where you interviewed yesterday. The only problem is, you're wearing baggy sweat pants with paint splatters, a T-shirt with the sleeves ripped out, and a baseball cap. Not a very good impression. But if you were dressed nicely, what a great opportunity to make another contact.

Don't feel you have to wear a suit all the time. When you leave the house, dress like casual day on Friday in an office. That way you're not embarrassed if you run into someone important—instead you can take advantage of the situation and use it in a positive way.

❧ Robin had just relocated to Colorado with her family and wanted an administrative position in a doctor's office. One day she was on her way to the grocery store when she noticed a family practice doctor's office nearby. A woman, obviously an employee on her break, was standing outside the back door enjoying the sunshine. Robin, freshly showered and nicely dressed in pressed khaki pants and white shirt, parked her car and walked over to the woman. She introduced herself, gave her thirty-second commercial, and asked if the office had any openings. The woman happened to be the manager and said, "Yes, we do have an opening. Can you come in tomorrow for an interview?" Robin was hired for the first job she targeted, close to home, with the salary she desired.

# Make Your Job Search a Full-Time Job.

Your job search IS A JOB, and you must treat it accordingly. That means work diligently on it every day, just as you would in a job. The rule of thumb is to spend forty hours a week on your job search if you are unemployed and twenty hours a week if you are currently employed.

Why should you spend that much time? Perhaps you wanted to use some time to paint the family room, or plant a garden. If you want to do some odd jobs, fine. But try to keep them confined to evenings and weekends.

You need to commit the time to your search—the more energy you put in, the more positive results you will receive, faster. You'll feel productive and knowledgeable by learning about your field, talking to people, and making contacts. The best benefit of this technique is being able to choose between job offers. If you perform your job search in an effective systematic way, you will probably enjoy multiple, simultaneous interviews. This creates a confident, enthusiastic demeanor in you, and the very desirable traits that employers look for. In turn, they are more likely to make job offers. Having several job offers to choose from is worth all the extra effort. After all, how many hours, weeks, months, and years are you going to spend in this job? Forty hours a week is small potatoes compared to the time on your new job.

For the average job hunter, it takes five interviews to render one job offer. By following the techniques outlined in this book, you can increase your chances. How long does it take to set up one interview? Five visits with contacts, thirty calls, and three letters? One study showed that if a job hunter contacted two employers a week, the job search typically lasted up to a year; if ten employers were contacted a week, the search typically lasted up to six months; and at twenty employers a week, the search time typically dropped to ninety days or less.*

How many weeks or months do you want to spend on your job search?

*(Goodrich & Sherwood Co., reported in "How to Succeed in Rotten Times," Oct. 1992)

# *Pursue Every Lead or Idea.*

Leave no stone unturned. You have already committed to spending forty hours a week (or twenty if you're currently employed) to your job search. That means you have plenty of time to investigate all leads. It's easy to discount an idea or lead if it comes from someone unorthodox or out of your respected field, like your car salesman brother-in-law or your biker neighbor. You just never know which path will lead to your ideal job.

❦ A woman looking for an executive assistant job found one through a lead from a friend in a stamp collecting group (the CEO who needed an assistant collected stamps, too).

❦ A top executive found a job through a lead from his wife via the Avon Lady.

❦ A loan officer found a job through a lead from his daughter's dog obedience class.

People may give you strange and unusual ideas. Try to have an open mind before automatically rejecting them; each is worth your consideration. If the idea is about unusual ways to research, by all means, go ahead and try it. It won't hurt anything. Perhaps a friend is coaxing you to try the internet as a job search method and you're not a computer person. Try it! It's just new to you.

However, avoid doing anything wacky that will turn off prospective employers. Try conservative methods first, then if that doesn't get results, try more unorthodox methods.

❦A mature man wanted a sales position for a particular company and couldn't get an interview. Desparate, he dressed in a dark pin-stripped suit and made up fake business cards identifying him as an IRS agent. He visited the vice president's office and demanded a meeting. He got the meeting, but as you can imagine, things went bad when he revealed his true identity and purpose.

❦A woman who wanted to be a concierge in a resort could not get an audience with the hiring manager through the usual channels. Her letters and phone calls went unanswered. She hired a concierge at the resort she was targeting and had her resume and short note delivered via the concierge to the hiring manager on a silver platter with a single red rose. She had to do this twice, but was granted an interview and a job.

## *Expect Rejections.*

No matter how smart and how hard you work in your job search, you will get rejections. They will come from all directions. Some people won't want to network with you, some people won't return your phone calls, some people will reject you after an interview. It's a fact of life in your job search.

For all those people who said "no," there are other people who will say "yes." Keep trying no matter what happens. Strive to reach the yes people. Keeping a positive mental attitude is paramount to your success. Just think of every "no" as putting you one step closer to a "yes."

Don't give up on the first "no," either. Any good salesperson will tell you to ignore each "no" and keep right on going with your presentation. Try another angle, ask questions, or change tactics. After giving it your best shot, accept the "no" (for now!) and move on— closer to the "YES!"

# Chapter Two

# A Winning
# Attitude

# Decide to Have a Positive, Enthusiastic Attitude.

An optimistic, eager attitude is contagious. You pass it on to your networking contacts, over the phone, in letters, and in interviews. People want to help you because you're so confident and enthusiastic—a person who knows what you want and where you're going. Have you ever met a charming, charismatic person? Didn't you feel good just being around them? Didn't you want to spend time with them, do stuff with them, or perhaps do something for them? We are all attracted to positive thinkers.

Employer surveys show that the number one attribute employers want is a positive, enthusiastic attitude. Many skills can be taught and knowledge learned, but it's almost impossible to change someone else's attitude.

But you *can* change your own attitude! And you can change it starting now. According to Anthony Robbins, author of *Awaken the Giant Within*, you can change your attitude by changing your behavior. If you *act* like an enthusiastic person, soon you will *be* an enthusiastic person. What do enthusiastic people do? How do they act?

Start with good posture, sitting and standing. Whenever you catch yourself slumping, straighten up. Walk briskly with a spring in your step, and hold your head high. In the morning, look yourself in the eye and repeat, "I have a positive mental attitude. I'm excited to begin another great day!" Keep repeating it until you feel excited and are speaking with enthusiasm. Jump up and down, wave your arms in the air, do a jig—whatever it takes to get you going. Throughout the day, if your attitude is lagging, say out loud, "I'm a positive, enthusiastic person. I'm confident in my ability to land a great job." Observe enthusiastic people you know, and imitate their behavior.

# Treat Your Job Search as an Opportunity to Enhance Your Life.

Think about it. Enriching, fulfilling work is a key factor to true happiness in your life. When you are performing work you love, you feel confident and excited. You feel alive and alert. You're aware of everything around you, you radiate warm feelings—and sleep well at night. Problems become an interesting challenge, not an insurmountable obstacle.

If you have never felt this way away about work before, think of a time when you felt on top of the world. It could be when you went white water rafting, won a bowling game, or helped your child build a go cart or plant a garden. You were laughing, having fun, and accomplishing important things. Imagine feeling that way about your job, *every day*.

Now is your opportunity to do something important—for you and your family. Searching for rewarding work is one of the most important jobs you can do. Do not treat it lightly. Take the time to ferret out the work you love, that uses your most valuable skills, experiences, and knowledge. Even if you have to go back to school or start in an entry level job, it will pay off in a big way in the future. By doing work you love, you will naturally excel and become the best in your field. Because you're intensely interested and excited about your work, you will care about it more, study it more, think of new and better ways to do it, and put in a little extra effort.

Bonus: Because you excel in your work, you will make more money and always be in demand.

# Conduct Everyday Activities as If You Are Working in a Real Job.

It's important to your self esteem to keep busy and keep a semblance of working during this time. Sleeping in and dressing sloppily are sure ways to counteract a positive attitude. Rise every morning at your normal time, and go through your usual morning routine. Shower, shave, fix your hair, put on make-up. You don't have to wear a suit every day, but wear something presentable, perhaps as you would wear on Casual Day at work.

Now, since you're prepared to work, work on your job search. The temptation is to start household chores, that project you've been meaning to do for months, or worse—daytime TV. Save chores, household projects, and TV for your leisure hours in the evenings or on weekends. Your number one project is your job search. The longer you put it off, the longer it will take to find a job. And finding your dream job takes a little extra effort.

If the house is distracting you, leave. Go to the library, and begin research on the industries and companies you are interested in. Or visit the career section, and find more good books on job search. Also check out the business newspapers. (See *Use the Library for Leads and Research*, p. 143.) Soon, networking and interviewing will take you out of the house. Some who people who work from a home office actually get in their car and drive around the block to make them feel like they are going to work.

Get up, get dressed for work, and work on your job search every day. It's important to establish this routine as a habit early in your job search. After a week or two, it becomes a beneficial habit that enhances your attitude as well as your progress.

# When You Are Feeling Down, Do Something Uplifting.

Go for a walk, see a funny movie, call a positive-attitude friend, play with your kids, read a motivational book, arrange flowers, work on your favorite hobby, or play with the cat. Do something to get you out of the "funk." Employers and networking contacts can sense when something's not right (when you are feeling down) and are less responsive to you. Shake this feeling at all costs.

❦ Ryan is a man who had more than his share of tragedy visit his life, yet he is one of the most positive-attitude people I know. The last straw was when his company downsized and he was let go. Yet through all of his troubles, he maintained a good outlook on life. I asked him how he did it. He said, "I made a list of all the things I am grateful for in my life and I read them out loud every day." Ryan's house burned down, his wife had a serious illness, he lost his job, and he still maintained a positive attitude. Needless to say, with his outlook and energy, he found a good job in a short period of time.

Another method for keeping the blues away is to exercise regularly. Your exercise program can take any shape or form such as gardening and landscaping, running or walking in a park, lifting weights at the gym, joining an aerobics class, playing tennis, riding a bicycle, or swimming. Be sure not to do this during your prime job search time unless you need an emergency uplifting. Or use it as a reward: "If I get all my tasks done by 4 p.m., I will go on a bike ride."

# *No One Owes You a Job.*

Sometimes we have a tendency to blame others for what is going wrong in our lives. And so it is with your job search. When you feel like you're taking two steps backward to one step forward, it's easy to point a finger at the recruiter, employment agency, your networking contacts, or your previous employer. The plain and simple truth is: No one cares as much about your job search as you do, no one will put as much loving attention into your job search as you can.

No one owes you a job no matter what your circumstances are, no matter how good you are at your work, and no matter who you know. The sooner you accept the fact that you have to find a job through your own efforts, rather than depending on others to do so, the sooner you will begin the real work of your job search and land a job.

It's fine to use recruiters and employment agencies, just don't use them as the primary, or sole, means for your job search. If you do the research, and you network with people about your industry and potential employers, you will learn much more about your specific job market and be able to choose a position and company that's better suited for you. And you will do it faster.

Ultimately, finding a job is your responsibility, and yours alone.

# Never Complain About Your Job Search.

When you complain about anything, it puts you, and your audience, in a negative state of mind. Some people may be sympathetic or even responsive to your job situation and the hardships you may be suffering. But the bottom line is, most people get very tired of hearing about someone else's problems and want to change the subject or get away from the complainer.

Occasionally, you need to talk to someone about the downfalls you may experience. Choose a trusted friend or spouse to talk with. Try to make it brief, and concentrate on the problem, don't just chronically complain. Ask for advice, and *listen* to your confidante's suggestions, and decide to do something about your mood. Action is the dispeller of depression. Even if you conclude there's nothing you can do about a particular situation, you can decide to let it go.

As I have mentioned, one of best tools at your disposal during your job search is your positive attitude. Maintaining your positive attitude can be difficult at times, but it is one of the key attributes employers look for. People with a positive attitude have that magic sparkle, a certain energy. One way to stay positive is to avoid complaining.

# *Maintain a Sense of Humor*

Not only am I asking you to have a positive attitude, I ask that you have a sense of humor, too! Is it asking too much? I don't think so. If you can laugh and maintain your humor, not only is it healthy for you, it demonstrates confidence and a casual poise that is attractive to employers.

Here are some ideas to help maintain your sense of humor:

- Read the comics everyday
- Watch cartoons on TV with your kids
- Read funny stories or comic books to your kids
- Read humorous books
- Read about job search blunders
- Rent funny movies or go to the theater
- Go see a live comedy show
- Enjoy stand-up comedians on HBO or cable specials
- Watch the comedy cable station

- Tune in to the monologues of Jay Leno and David Letterman
- Visit with a witty, humorous friend
- Read joke books
- Learn to tell jokes well
- Watch sports bloopers
- Watch *America's Funniest Home Videos*
- Do whatever makes you laugh

# *Avoid Discrimination.*

One of the most common questions job hunters ask me is, "What can I do about age discrimination?" My answer is that you have to look at the root of the question and address the real issue. In the case of age, it probably isn't "age" the employer is concerned about but issues that may be associated with age. The employer is thinking: Will I have to pay him more money than I planned due to his experience? Does he have medical problems? Is she energetic enough to keep up with the job? Can she use our computer system? Will she get along with young people?

Knowing the issues the employer is concerned about will help you turn it around. Address it up front. List computer skills on your resume (or take classes to update your skills), be energetic on the phone and in person, during the interview give examples of working with young people, and mention your healthy lifestyle. Of course, your appearance will probably answer health concerns. Salary is usually negotiable and depends on your standards and your ability to negotiate. (See *Negotiate for Top Dollars*, p. 201.)

What about the *benefits* of being older? Older employees are more mature, dependable, and responsible, they have years of experience and knowledge to put to use and won't make rash decisions. Mature employees know what they want, and won't leave on a whim.

This example can serve with just about any type of discrimination you think may face you: age, color, race, sex, religion, etc. And, of course, there are real down and dirty cases of discrimination. My advice is to address the real issues and try to overcome the objectives. If that doesn't work, then go on to other employers. Whatever your issue may be, there are employers out there that *will hire you*.

Your mission is to find those employers.

# Motivate Yourself.

Of all your job search tasks, this is often the hardest to do. If you learn to motivate yourself, and do it on a daily basis, you can overcome any obstacle. Action is the friend of motivation and the enemy of depression.

Start a daily routine as soon as possible, and adhere to it every day whether you feel like it or not. After a week, it becomes a habit, a very good habit. Each person's routine will be different, but it should include waking up at a reasonable time, eating breakfast, grooming and dressing for work, and completing your planned job search tasks for the day.

Exercise is extremely helpful to relieve anxiety, keep your body in shape, and your mind alert. Continue or increase your exercise program if you already have one. If you haven't exercised up until now, begin! Walking is the easiest exercise to start. All you need is some good walking shoes. Take it easy, and build up a little every day.

Another great way to motivate yourself is to listen to success tapes and motivational speakers. Visit your local bookstore for a selection, and invest in several. Listen to them whenever you are in your car, or while you're walking. It's hard to feel down when you're listening to uplifting people. Besides audio tapes, you can talk to successful, uplifting people. Call your positive-attitude friends on a regular basis; meet them for lunch.

Do not watch daytime television. It's easy to get sucked into that dark hole where you don't have to think or do anything. Keep the TV off all day—you have work to do!

Do not start major projects that will take over your days. This is another mistake some job hunters make. They get tied up in remodeling, painting the house, and landscaping. How much time do you want to spend looking for a job? If you plan to stay home and do major projects, fine, just don't kid yourself that you are job hunting. Save the projects for evenings and weekends.

# Chapter Three

# Remarkable Resumes
and Cover Letters

# Emphasize Accomplishments, Skills, and Results in Your Resume.

Far too many resumes are a boring list of vague responsibilities and duties. So what? Who cares what you were *supposed* to do? The employer wants to know how you *performed* those duties. Sure, the scope of your responsibilities is important, but *how* you did them is twice as important. What were your objectives on a certain project or job? What skills did you use to achieve them? What were the results? That's what the employer wants to know.

Accomplishments are things you have done that create value, often improving the profitability of the company in some way. Here are some examples: generated revenue, cut costs, saved time, increased productivity, improved customer service, motivated or trained or taught others, invented or created, improved quality, and used technology. Write your accomplishments in brief sentences starting with an action verb and stating results whenever possible. Eliminate these words: I, we, duties, and responsibilities. The practice will help you write more concise and descriptive phrases. Examples:

- Recruited, trained, and motivated a sales force of eight people. Increased sales by 27% in one year.
- Planned and orchestrated a Grand Opening Gala with 1,500 people attending. Project was within budget and boosted positive image of company.
- Restructured filing system assuring streamline retrieval of files and saving five filing hours per week.

We are a numbers driven country. Use numbers whenever possible to describe results. Use percentages and dollar amounts, whichever best suit your description. Express numbers in a way that make the biggest impact such as: $85,000 instead of $85K or $1.5 million instead of $1,500,000 or 30% increase instead of a $2,000 increase, or $300,000 increase instead of a 5% increase. Use percent signs and numerical figures in your resume to make it easier to read, but not in written correspondence.

If your accomplishment doesn't have a numerical result, then describe the *benefits* derived from your actions (mediated hostile situation, saved time, made patients feel at ease, etc.).

# *Create an Outstanding Profile.*

The profile is an extremely important section of your resume. Placed at the top of your resume, it's the first thing employers will read; they will either trash it or continue reading based on what it says. It can also be called a Summary or Qualifications. It is a thumbnail sketch of why you are qualified to do the job you are seeking. Only information relevant to your objective should be included here, or in your entire resume for that matter. A profile may include your best characteristics, years of experience, special skills, plus education, licenses, or training required for the job.

It should be written in bullet style beginning with an action verb. Four or five lines is sufficient.

Ask yourself, "What is the employer looking for?" Imagine that you are the employer—your next boss. What kind of qualities would you want in the ideal candidate? What key personality characteristics should this candidate possess? Some examples are team player, ability to work alone, reliable, enthusiastic, accurate, humane, results oriented, outgoing, and organized. Obviously, a salesperson will have a different personality than a lab technician.

How much experience, training, and education should the ideal candidate have?

Now, match your qualifications as closely as possible to the qualifications the employer desires. These are your "hot buttons." You will use them over and over in your job search in letters, networking, on the phone, and in interviews. Know them well.

# *State a Clear Objective.*

Many people say, "I don't want to be tied down to an objective. I want to be open to any job." The people who take the longest in a job search are the ones who don't know what they want. If you can't write out your objective, then you don't know what you want. Your entire resume (and job search) is based on your objective. The employer doesn't have time to wade through your resume and say "Oh gosh, what a nice person! We must have something here this person can do." Sorry, it won't happen. YOU have to decide what you want to do.

Being flexible is desirable. You may even have two or three objectives and resumes to match. That is the best way to target several job search areas. Another way is to express your objective while retaining flexibility is to identify it by function and industry. For instance Sales/Aircraft or Office Management/Family Practice or Electrician/Custom Homes or Events Coordinator for Tennis/Golf Sporting Events.

If you simply can't figure out what you want to do, you must perform more research and self-assessment before you begin a job search. Visit a career counselor at your local community college to see if career exploratory classes are available. If you are a student, the counselor can give you some tests to help guide you. Also, go to the library or bookstore and browse through the job hunting section. *JobFinder: How to Find a Better Job Faster,* also by Claudia Jordan, has an entire appendix just for this topic with exercises and questions to help you.

# Short Resumes Sell.

Employers do not have time to read lengthy resumes. They want to glean as much as possible from your resume with a glance, then a few minutes of reading. That's why your profile and objective are so important- -they let the employer know who and what you are in about thirty-seconds—the average time an employer looks at your resume the first time.

Here are some interesting findings about resume length from a survey by the placement firm of Robert Half International.

- Sixty-four percent of executives believe the preferable length for an *executive* resume is two pages.
- Seventy-three percent of executives believe the preferable length for a *staff-level* resume is one page.

The body of the resume is what most people overload. You do not have to include everything you've ever done. Go back only about ten years. If you really must mention positions before that, you can list them under "Previous Experience" and just name the positions or positions and companies. Was there a job you held less than a year? Just eliminate it. For employment dates, you should list only years, without months, to make it easier to read and hide small gaps.

Under each job, list only your best accomplishments that are relevant to your new job target. If it's not relevant, drop it. It's just extra baggage. After you have finished writing, go back over the resume and see if you can say the same things using less words. Shorten phrases and sentences wherever possible. Use a thesaurus to find the strongest, most descriptive words. Writing in short phrases will deliver punch and pizzazz!

# Make Your Resume Look Like a Winner.

A top-notch resume pays attention to appearance, grammar, printing, and style. It must pass the "scan test" from employers, entice them to read more, and call you.

Use good-quality stationery in a neutral color such as cream, white, or pale gray. It should match the envelope unless you send it in a 10 x 13-inch envelope. Use only black ink for printing. The overall appearance should include: at least a one-inch margin on the sides and one-half inch at the top and bottom, type that is not too big and not too small (eleven or twelve point), and name, address, and phone at the top. It should be one or two pages in length.

Make sure the following items are easy to find and read: objective, profile, job titles, names of companies, years worked, and education. These items should be well organized and have matching headings. The achievements from each position are written in bullet style making it a simple feat for the employer to pick out a couple and read them.

Grammar and punctuation should be perfect. Many resumes are dumped because of a typo or poor grammar. Proofread your materials. Use a dictionary, and then have several other people who are good with grammar read your resume. If you use a computer, always use spell check, but be sure to proofread also. The spell check cannot tell you to use "two" instead of "to" or "there" instead of "their," etc.

If you are in an artistic field, such as graphic design, you will want to have a more creative resume presentation. Ask your associates, or check out the library for some examples in your field.

Don't have access to a computer to create your resume and correspondence? See *Get Organized*, p. 21 for alternative solutions.

Posting your resume on the internet requires a different sort of resume. Employers search resumes using nouns rather than verbs. Think of what the employer will punch in for search words, such as names of software/computer programs, specific training, licenses, certification, or degree. List as many relevant nouns as you can in your resume, and forget the fancy typesetting.

# *Personalize Your Cover Letter.*

Do you like getting junk mail addressed to "Resident"? Neither do employers. If you don't take the time to find out their name, why should they take the time to interview you? Will you treat their customers or employees with the same indifference? Or work on projects without caring about attention to detail?

This is your job, your life. The little extra work you do now will pay off later. With that said, how do you find the name of the person with whom you want to interview?

This person should be your next boss. He or she is the one who will make the hiring decision, and that's who you should target. The easiest way to get the name is to call the company and ask. "Who is in charge of the _____ department?" "Who is the vice president of _____?" "What is the name of your manager, supervisor, owner, or regional manager?" You don't have to talk to that person, just ask the name, its spelling, the person's title, and company address. If it's a generic name like Pat or Chris ask if the person is a Ms. or Mr. If asked why you want the name, (and you probably won't be) just say you're sending a letter or some information.

You can also find names from networking and research. If you obtain a name this way, still call the company and verify name, spelling, title, and address. In some cases, such as want ads with P.O. boxes, getting the name of the person is impossible. Make every effort to get a name or title, then as a last resort use, "Dear Selection Committee" or the company's name or a title.

If you are faxing your resume, be sure to use a cover letter, and address the decision maker who would hire you, then mail a copy, too.

# Construct a Winning Cover Letter.

A cover letter should always accompany your mailed, e-mailed, or faxed resume. Every contact you make with the employer is an opportunity to make a good impression. Tailor key points to a specific topic or position, use research to demonstrate your knowledge of the company and industry, and address special issues like a gap in your work history, change of career, or relocation.

A cover letter is written in standard business style. It is typed, has your name, address, and phone at the top, indicates the name, title, company, and address of the person to whom you are writing. It includes the date, a salutation such as Dear Mr. or Ms._____:, the body of the letter and the closing, such as Sincerely or Cordially.

The first paragraph of the letter is the introduction and should tell the recipient why you are writing and give him or her a compelling reason to read on. If you have the name of a referral, always use it in the first sentence. Otherwise, let the reader know how you heard of the company or position.

"Tom Anderson from XYZ Company suggested getting in touch with you about ..." or "According to industry sources, McKay Enterprises is planning to introduce a new line of widgets..." or "In the July 7th issue of *The Business Journal,* Blue Mountain Resort was mentioned..." or "I saw your ad in the *Denver Post...*"

The second paragraph or body of the cover letter is the sales pitch. Why should the employer hire YOU? What do you offer that no one else has? This is sometimes called your Unique Selling Position—your special blend of personality, experience, and knowledge. Demonstrate your knowledge of the company and the industry using research information. Do this by sharing relevant top accomplishments, skills, and knowledge you possess to help solve the company's specific problems or challenges. Show your qualifications for the position and the benefits you could bring to the company.

The closing should restate your enthusiasm for the job and indicate what action is to happen next. The most effective is to state you will call to make an appointment for a meeting. Be sure to follow through or you will cause more damage than good. Following up with a phone call increases your chances of a meeting by fifty percent. Your cover letter should not exceed one page.

# *Don't Mention Salary in a Resume or Cover Letter.*

It will probably screen you *out* of the running for the job.

Salary history should never be mentioned in a resume. You *should* mention figures to show the scope of your position, but not salary. Good examples are: "Sold $19.5 million in real estate..." or "Managed budget of $750,000..." However, mentioning your salary can very well screen you out because it is too high or too low. Before you get screened out for that, you want a chance to meet face-to-face to negotiate for higher pay.

Discussion of pay should always be saved for the end of an interview and then only after serious hiring interest is shown. (See *Negotiate for Top Dollars*, p. 201.) If you must fill out an application, fill in the "Salary required" blank with "negotiable."

Salary requirements and history should not appear in your cover letter, either, for all the same reasons. In seminars, people always ask me, "But some want ads ask for salary history/requirements, and they won't read your letter unless you list it. How do you handle that?"

Instead of mentioning a figure, say your salary is proportionate to your responsibilities, or within industry standards, plus bonuses, profit sharing, etc. Or that you will be happy to discuss salary in an interview. Another tactic is to express it in a range such as low forties. Don't even think of doing this unless the ad specifically asks for salary history or requirements and you think you would be screened out without it.

It is to your advantage not to mention a figure at all.

## *Proofread Your Written Materials Meticulously.*

Many employers use typos and poor grammar to screen out applicants. Why should they bother with someone who can't bother to spell words correctly? Remember that everything you do in your job search is a reflection of you and how well you will perform your future work.

Your resume and every letter you write need to be checked and rechecked for spelling, poor grammar, and typos. After you think they are perfect, have someone else look at them, preferably someone who is proficient in grammar. The problem is that each of us makes small mistakes without even realizing it. That's why you need other people to proofread for you. That's why writers have editors!

If you use a computer, always use spell check, but don't rely entirely on it. You still must read everything. Spell check checks spelling but not the correct use of words. It also helps to put the written material away and read it hours later or the next day.

Do you use the same words over and over? I once saw a resume with the word "managed" repeated sixteen times! A rule of thumb is to never use the same word twice. Look up words in the thesaurus for better descriptions and a livelier read.

# Use Your Resume and Cover Letter to Gain Interviews.

The best way to set up interviews is to *not* use your resume and cover letter. If you don't use a resume and cover letter, how will you make appointments for an interview? You would have to talk to the people in your network and set up appointments through your contacts. Or you would have to call employers and discuss why they should meet with you. And the last way would be to walk directly into the place you want to work and ask to talk to person in charge of what you want to do. Sound wild? It's not. These are the most successful ways to find a job.

Then why should you go to the trouble of writing a resume? Sooner or later the employer will ask you for one. Hopefully, it's after the interview, after you've already left a positive impression. The other reason to create a well-written resume is to organize and focus your thoughts to prepare *yourself* for a face-to-face meeting or a telephone discussion.

So, the best way to use a resume is after an interview. If you can't schedule a meeting any other way, then mail a resume and cover letter, or mail it first then follow up with phone calls. Faxing a resume is acceptable *when it's requested*, and always fax a cover letter with it. Remember, your cover letter lets you cover a lot more ground than a plain resume. I recommend mailing your resume/cover letter after you fax it because the printed version on rich stationery is more impressive, plus you've made contact twice.

To draw attention to your resume package, try mailing it in a white 10 x 13-inch envelope marked URGENT. Also try mailing it in a Priority Mail envelope from the post office or two-day mail from UPS or Federal Express. It's more expensive, but guaranteed to be read and make an impression. How about having your resume package hand delivered by a courier? (One of your friends, who can also give you the inside scoop.)

# Make a Follow-Up Call After Sending Your Resume.

After mailing your resume and cover letter, call within two days of its arrival. It will increase your chances of winning a meeting by fifty percent.

You should be able to estimate when it will arrive whether you're mailing it locally or out of town. Call within two days while your name is still fresh in the employer's mind. Ask if the employer has received your letter and if not, be prepared to tell her basically what your letter said. Then ask for a meeting. "I'd like to meet with you to discuss your expansion (new line of products, career opportunities, special services, etc.). Would Wednesday or Thursday be better for you?" Giving a choice of two times is better than a choice of yes or no. You may have to ask several times. "I understand you don't have any openings right now, but I'd still like to meet with you. I'll only take up twenty minutes of your time..."

Sometimes its hard to reach the decision maker by phone. If you get voice mail or the assistant, leave a brief message mentioning you sent your resume, that you want to make sure they received it and would like to set up a short meeting. Try calling in a couple of days, leaving only your name, and after a week leave your full message again. How persistent you are depends on the position and what kind of response you're getting.

# *Do Not Lie, Exaggerate, or Be Modest.*

As you look through the want ads, suddenly you spot the perfect job for you. Reading the description, your accomplishments match their requirements very well—except for that one little thing. A degree. Or a year or two of experience. It would be so easy just the fudge a little on your resume. You think, "I can do that job very well. What does it matter if I tell a little white lie? No one checks on these things." Wrong! Employers are so concerned with getting the right employee, they will check. Even if you manage to get the job, many people have been fired down the line when the truth surfaces. Don't do it.

You are right if you believe you are a close match and can perform the job well. Instead of lying, convince them of your abilities and confidence. Some positions require a degree or special training and there's no way to get around it. Would you want a surgeon to operate on you without the proper credentials? Unless the training or education is required by law or a license, treat new hire requirements as guidelines. These are the dream requirements the employer wants, and the more you have, the better. You may be able to overcome a weakness in one area with strengths from another. In your letter, or better yet in person, address these issues by emphasizing your strengths and confidence in your abilities. Don't point out what you are lacking.

There is a fine point between exaggerating and coming across as arrogant, being modest and looking like an underachiever, and expressing confident views of yourself. Confidence reins supreme. Exaggerating or being too modest will lose you the job. Stick with the facts, but express the facts in the most favorable way. Liken it to a flattering photograph of yourself. It's still you, but looking your very best.

# Chapter Four

# Networking
# Know-How

# *Create a Thirty-Second "Commercial."*

This is your opportunity to communicate clearly and confidently what you want so others can help you. People generally want to help you if you are specific about what you want and you communicate in a friendly, positive fashion. Your thirty-second commercial is essential in networking and becomes even more important when you begin calling employers and talking with them in person.

Basically, the thirty-second commercial tells what position and industry you're interested in and why you're qualified for that work. Your qualifications can be experience, education, skills, and personality—whatever your best points are. Most of this is already done if you have created a resume using this book. Use your objective and a few points from your profile.

A sample script would be, "Hello, my name is Jim Kelly. I'm looking for a position as a _____ in the _____ field. " My special skills are _____, _____, and _____,

and I have five years experience in _____. Do you know any-one in this field?"

If you can't explain the work you're targeting in one sentence, it's because you haven't clarified what you want to do. Go back to the beginning few chapters under Strategies and review. Also, look though the want ads to get an idea of names of positions that interest you.

Practice your script until it becomes natural to you, then begin networking with friends and relatives, and later, employers.

❧ Heather had just graduated from an interior design school. After targeting several companies, she walked into the one she wanted most with her portfolio in hand. It was lunch time, and the receptionist was gone, but there was a man behind the desk searching for something. Heather approached the man, used her thirty-second commercial and asked if anyone was available to meet with her. The man said, "Everyone is out to lunch, but I'm the president, and I rarely get to interview new people. Let's go in the conference room, and you can show me your portfolio." She was hired by the president.

# *Design Networking Cards.*

A networking card is a business-size card that you use to tell the world what kind of work you are seeking. Adding a few lines about your top qualifications will help people remember you and entice them to call you.

This special card should contain (from top to bottom): your name and phone number(s), your objective or the type of work you're seeking, and three or four of your best qualifications for the work.

Your address isn't necessary for this project, but your phone number is important. Make sure you can be reached easily or that people can leave a message, which you should return promptly. Your objective or description of the work you're seeking needs to be very clear. Your card should communicate the fact that you are *seeking work,* or it will look like just another business card. Use the words, "Job Objective," "Career Objective," "Job Target" or "Seeking a position as a _____." Next are three or four of your best qualifications for the target work. You have already outlined these in the profile section of your resume, so just lift a couple of lines from that. (See *Create an Outstanding Profile*, p. 63.) These points should cover any necessary degrees, licenses, or training; how much experience you have (if limited, leave it out); one or two accomplishments or awards; and a personality line suited to your work. Choose your strongest few points, but don't crowd the card. You want to entice them to call you, not read your life history.

You can have the cards printed at a copy/print shop. Make a nice presentation, but it need not be lavish. Compare prices with different paper stock and colors. Black ink on white paper is fine as long as the card is laid out in an attractive manner and says the right things.

Always carry your networking cards with you, and hand them out to everyone you meet. Send them to your relatives, friends, and neighbors. Put them in all the mail correspondence that leaves your house.

# *Line Up Your References.*

Now that you've defined the work you want to do and made networking cards, it's time to get your references on board. References are very important people in the job search; they can give a potential employer a glowing report, AND they can provide valuable job leads for you. Most people overlook the second aspect of their references, missing out on a premium way to make contacts and gather information. Your references know you and your work well and are in the best position to recommend you to others.

Start by making a list of your possible references. You need a minimum of three names, and four to five is average. The best references are former bosses or prestigious people in your field or community. Next would be people you have worked with closely such as customers, vendors, and associates. If you still need more references, co-workers and friends can be added, but unless they are prominent in your industry they will get little notice.

Now, add their titles, company names, addresses, and phone numbers. Call them and give them your thirty-second commercial, and ask if they will be your reference. Most people are flattered to help. Verify their job titles and phone numbers. At the end of your conversation, ask if they know of any new developments in your field or any job leads. NEVER ask your reference for a job—they will volunteer that information if they feel comfortable about it. Thank them for their time.

The references should be listed on a separate sheet of paper, which matches the style of your resume, with your name, address, and phone number at the top. Type REFERENCES, and list them. Noting your relationship to the reference is helpful to the potential employer doing a background check. If a former supervisor is currently working in a different position, or company, than when you worked for them, make a note of it.

Write a letter to each reference stating what kind of work you're seeking, and thank the recipient again for his help. Mention that you'll be in touch and that you would appreciate hearing from them if they learn new information about your field. Enclose your resume (if an employer calls they can refer to it) and several networking cards.

Potential employers want to verify how you perform your work and what kind of person you are. Your list of references is a valuable tool to potential employers since so many companies will only verify name, rank, and serial number. Supplying your references is to your advantage because you're certain you'll get glowing recommendations from everyone on your list since you have previously talked with each of them.

Do not mail your reference list with your resume unless it is long distance or requested. Why needlessly bother your references with extra calls or add extra papers to your presentation? Hand out your reference sheet only after an interview for a job you want to pursue. After the interview, hand it to the employer, and invite him to call your references, who are standing by. This is a great way to use your list to show how professional and organized you are—you can even use it to close the sale.

An alternative is to get a letter of recommendation from an employer you are leaving, before you leave. If someone, such as your boss is willing to write the letter, it's always good to have for your files.

Call every couple of weeks to chat with your references and mention who may be calling them or get feedback from a background check. Offer them any new insights you have gleaned that may be helpful to them, and ask if they have any industry news or job leads for you. If you can develop an exchange of information with key contacts, such as your references, it will help you tremendously. Inside information to which you may be privy from your research, networking, and interviewing includes new products, new companies, promotions, industry salaries, mergers, sell-outs, relocations, and expansions, etc.

❦ Jake was looking for a position as a purchasing agent in the electronics field. After being an electronic sales rep for years, he tired of it and wanted to switch to the other side of the table. He decided to contact his references. He called a former boss (from seven years prior), told him of his career path and asked him to be his reference. The former boss gave him a lead—a recruiter who was looking for a purchasing agent. Jake contacted the recruiter, went through a series of seven interviews, and landed his dream job.

# Build a Network.

Of all the jobs filled today, seventy to eighty percent are filled by word-of-mouth. Networking is the most valuable and effective method you can use to find a good job. You can't afford not to do it.

You know many more people than you think you do. Start with ten friends and relatives and tell them what you want to do using your thirty-second commercial. Elaborate a little, explain why you decided on this particular position, and why you'd be good at it. Ask if they know anyone who does the kind of work that you are interested in, or who works in a company that does this kind of work, or the names of companies that perform this kind of work. If one of your initial contacts gives you a name to call, ask if you can mention his or her name when you phone the new contact.

When you call the new contact, mention the person who referred you and recite your thirty-second commercial. Add that you're exploring career opportunities. Ask if they would meet with you briefly or talk on the telephone about: 1) their expertise and knowledge in their particular field, 2) their company that does the type of work you're seeking (even though they have a different type of job there), 3) their advice on how to strategize your job campaign, 4) names of companies that do the kind of work you are targeting, 5) the names of anyone else who may help you.

Be flexible about where and when you can meet with them or set aside time to talk on the telephone. If the contact will meet you in her office, so much the better to get an inside view. Once you have a meeting set up, stick to your twenty minutes, and ask good questions. (See *Ask Good Questions*, p. 99.)

After you have finished talking to your initial list of ten people, it's time to expand. Add names from your Christmas/Holiday card list, your church, organizations, associations, and clubs to which you belong, past and present. Look in your address book, and add more names: acquaintances, co-workers past and present, and neighbors. Don't forget to add your doctor, dentist, lawyer, and banker. And how about your hairstylist, manicurist, landscaper, housecleaner, pest control person, car mechanic, grocer, and mail carrier? The idea is to inform everyone you know or meet, communicate the kind of work that you're seeking, pass out your networking card, and get a referral.

# Network with Out-of-State Contacts.

It is indeed a small world. It has been said that any individual is only seven people away from any other person in the United States. Networking does work, whether it be local, out-of-town, or out-of-state. And today, with the internet and e-mail, people keep in touch with lightning speed.

❦ Cindy had relocated to a different state and after three years decided to change professions from real estate to retail store management, her previous occupation. Her first step was to contact her former boss to ask him to be a reference. She had not spoken to him for more than three years. When he found out that she wanted to get back to retail management, he said, "Cindy, that's great! Did you know that, as we speak, our company is negotiating to buy six stores in your state? If it goes through, we'd love to have you back on board." The deal went through and Cindy was instrumental as the regional manager since she had lived in the state three years.

❧ Mary was re-entering the job market after her children started school and decided to target an accounting job. Her career counselor recommended that she start networking, but Mary was so shy, she was embarrassed to tell anyone. Finally, the counselor suggested that she tell at least one person: her brother who lived in California, several states away. When the brother learned of her decision to be an accountant, he recommended a friend he knew in her hometown, and Mary got the job.

❧ Tom was seeking a position as a technical writer. He had been looking for a long time and was about to give up. One day his father was talking to the tree trimmer he had hired. The father told the tree trimmer of his son's job search. The tree trimmer said, "My wife heads up a technical writing group, and she's looking for a writer." The wife interviewed the son (who lived in another state), and he was hired for a job he loved, in a location he loved.

## *Ask Good Questions.*

The questions you ask your networking contacts will vary depending on the level of the contact. Once you have recited your thirty-second commercial, start asking questions. Do you know people who work in my field? Do you know anyone who works in a company that does the work I'm seeking? Do you know the names of any companies or businesses that do the work I'm seeking? Do you have any ideas that may help me in my job search? Have you heard of any opportunities, industry trends, or newsworthy items about my profession? Do you know anyone who knows a lot of people?

Gather as much information as possible from each contact, and especially try to get at least two referrals from each person. When you are talking with someone doing the kind of work you want or working in a company you're interested in, ask these questions: How did you get your job? How did you break into this field? What do you like the most/least about your job? What is your greatest challenge? What is your company like? What is the management like? What professional publications in this industry should I read? What professional organizations are relevant to this profession or industry? Who are the recognized leaders in this industry? What is a typical career path for someone with my experience? Do you think my skills and knowledge would benefit this company? Is there training for this type of work? Do you know other professionals I should contact? What is the name of the person who hires for this position? May I use your name when contacting people you recommended?

These questions, and yours as your develop them, will give you insights into specific companies, how to approach them, more job leads, and produce more contacts.

Your contacts are valuable people and should be treated with the utmost courtesy. If you get the feeling you are pushing too hard, back off. Always be polite, professional, and brief while developing rapport. Genuine respect and interest nurture relationships. People are usually flattered that you're interested in them and their advice. Since you are pursuing a field you love, you generate enthusiasm and keen interest naturally.

# Get the Most Out of Networking.

People like hearing stories. Think of a funny story or insight that happened to you in your job search and tell people about it. It will allow them to relax around you, especially if it's a humorous story or one in which you can laugh at yourself a little. If you have stories about specific companies, products, or services your acquaintance may be interested in, don't hesitate to share them.

When people find out you're looking for work, often there is a little tension. They feel uncomfortable and awkward because they don't know what to say, or if you'll ask them for a job. Generally, they don't want to get bogged down in your gloom. When you tell them a story or an interesting fact, they are secretly relieved that they don't have to go through the empathetic, emotional stuff. They relax and are more open to you. If you are interesting (and especially upbeat) they think, "Wow, she really has her act together. Perhaps I could help in some small way..."

You can take this situation one step farther and offer something of value to the people you meet. It can be a small thing. An exchange of information is perfect. You must really listen to each person, and ask questions to discover what might help them. It may be a person or service you refer to them, an article clipped out and mailed to them, or a juicy tidbit about a competitor.

# *Never Ask Your Contacts for a Job.*

Asking friends, acquaintances, or contacts for a job makes them uncomfortable. They aren't sure if you are the right person for the job, and they don't want to put their necks on the line by hiring you or recommending you. A new contact is even more leery if you ask him for a job. If you can't ask these contacts for a job, then why network? Isn't that the point—to get a job through networking?

There is an art to networking. Most of the time, your aim is to spread the word about your job search, and gather information, suggestions, job leads, and referrals. When you get closer to your target work, your tactics will change. When you want your contact to refer you to the person who has the power to hire you, your approach will include more of your qualifications for the job and what you can do for the company. You must convince your contact that you are a good candidate for the job and the company. Once you have gleaned enough information about the company to apply for the job, you can call your contact and ask her to set it up, refer you, or if you may at least use her name when you call. (See *Arrange Interviews Through Your Contacts*, p. 113.)

The rule of thumb is to never ask your contacts for a job. You risk alienating them. Instead ask for suggestions, referrals, and job leads. If they want to interview you for a job or recommend you for a job, they will volunteer to do so if they are convinced you are a good candidate for the job.

When you are ready to meet with the person who can hire you for your target job, fine tune your approach. (See Chapter Six: *Ace the Interview,* p. 159.)

# *Ask Each Contact for Two Referrals.*

Without networking, you are one person alone looking for job leads. It will take a long time to find a good job. The more eyes and ears you have looking for you, the greater your chances are of finding a great job, and the sooner it will happen.

Let's say you start your networking list with ten friends and relatives, and you get two referrals from each person. After you talk to the new contacts, that equals thirty people who know you are in the job market and what job you want. If the second group of twenty people each gives you two referrals (forty more names), and you talk with them, you now have seventy people keeping their eyes and ears open for job leads for you. Let's take it one step farther. The third group gives you two referrals each (eighty more names), and you talk to each of them. Now you have a total of 150 people from whom to draw job leads!

Remember, seventy to eighty percent of all jobs are filled by word-of-mouth and are never advertised. And these tend to be the better jobs.

Ask each contact for two referrals. ("Do you know someone else I might speak with?") Most people can handle that. Some will give you more, some will give you less. But it's up to you to ask and follow through.

Keep your network strong by eventually weeding out the people who are not helpful to you and keeping in regular contact with those who are.

# *Discover New Leads Through Professional Associations.*

Professional and trade associations can open doors to industry news, rumors, new contacts, and job leads. People are friendlier and easier to approach in a more casual setting, and where else can you meet so many good contacts in one place?

Find the appropriate associations by asking contacts in your field or at the library in the *Encyclopedia of Associations*. Before you go, do a little background work on the association by talking with a member you know or contacting the association and asking for its brochure and membership materials. Ask for a membership roster, too (*very* helpful!). Some will provide it, some won't unless you are a member. Armed with information, head for the meeting. Don't forget your networking cards. (See *Design Networking Cards*, p. 89.)

Your aim is to meet new contacts, learn of job leads and hear industry news. Use finesse when meeting people. The last thing you want to do in this kind of situation is bludgeon people over the head with your job search. Think of some tidbits of information you can share with others, making your interaction more like an exchange of ideas and information. Do hand out your networking card to everyone you meet, everyone at your table, and leave some on the brochure table. Your cards spell out that you're in the job market and describe your target job. On the back of the cards you receive, write the date and event as well as why you'll call or write later.

Try to obtain a membership list at the meeting. The membership list is a gold mine of excellent sources of employers. Approach these employers in person at the meeting or future meetings, call them if appropriate, and/or send a personalized letter with your resume.

If you want to go the extra mile, join the association and volunteer to be on the membership committee—you'll make a lot of contact with the members.

The association you choose doesn't have to be your job target's trade or industry. Leads come from all people. A non-industry association may be very helpful *because* you're the only one from your field.

# *Send Thank-You Notes to Everyone Who Helps You.*

People love getting personal mail and especially love receiving a thank-you note for a small, kind deed they performed. Luckily for you, most people never bother to perform this small gesture so your note will stand out like an oasis in the desert. When was the last time you received a thank-you note? How did it make you feel?

Invest in a large stock of tasteful thank-you notes and stamps. Send hand-written notes to everyone who helps you in any way. Each networking contact who refers you to other people, produces a job lead, makes a good suggestion, provides helpful information, or simply gives you a few minutes of her time, should receive a thank-you note. Don't forget the gatekeepers—administrative assistants, secretaries, receptionists, and executive assistants. Incidentally, they can be very helpful in referring other people to you as well as helping you to meet with their boss. Making a second contact through your note helps them to remember you. You may be calling this person again during your job search and you want him to remember you with good feelings. *Always* enclose your networking card along with your note. (See *Design Networking Cards*, p. 89.)

Thank-you notes should be mailed within twenty four hours of your contact with each person. Make it a habit to write them out every night. (Remember to get people's business cards or company name to look up the address later.) In the note, mention how you met the recipient and specifically how he or she was helpful to you.

In addition to your thank-you note, a good way to follow up with contacts is to call them and share the results of their help. Examples: how the article they sent you helped you, the results of your calling the people they referred to you, how their suggestion about a job search strategy worked out, your research on a company they recommended to you, how their insight helped you in an interview, etc.

These thank-you notes are not to be confused with the letter you send after an interview. That should be a typed business letter stating key hiring points. (See *Send a Thank-You Letter After an Interview*, p. 197.)

# Keep a File of Your Network Contacts.

Keeping track of and organizing your contacts is important if you want to stay on top of the situation and reap the best results. The most effective ways to organize yourself are to use 3 x 5-inch cards and an index box, or a computer file that allows you to make detailed notes.

Sort your contacts into three levels, A, B, and C. Level A will be your best and most helpful contacts, B somewhat helpful, and C not helpful but you have made contact with them. Write each person's name, address, and phone number and any personal information you have such as who referred you to him, where he works and his position, his interests, hobbies, or names of spouse and children. Make notes of dates and conversations, meetings, and correspondence. Before calling or meeting a contact, pull out her card and review it. Break the ice by asking about her child or golf game (or whatever applies to that person).

Review your contact file weekly to plan your follow-up with contacts and refresh your memory. Jot down in your daily planner when to call people back.

The network you are building is not just until you find a job. Smart, successful people have a cache of contacts and practice networking as a life-long skill. Why not join the club?

# *Arrange Interviews Through Your Contacts.*

Networking is about building relationships. Once you have cultivated relationships with key people in your network and have impressed them as a confident, sharp professional with attainable goals—well, who wouldn't want to help you?

Having a contact call and set up a meeting/interview with the decision maker for you is the best possible situation you can hope for. That is why you work so hard to build and nurture your network! Many companies pay their employees for referrals. The next best situation is to use the contact's name when you call or write to the decision maker. Never use a contact's name without his or her permission.

After you have a list of companies to target, the next step is to find out the name of the person who would hire you (probably your boss if you worked there). Talk to your network and ask if they know anyone who works at your targeted companies, then meet with *that* person to learn more about the company and get the name of the hiring person. Or you may already have met with an employee of a targeted company. In that case, call him and ask the name of the person who would hire you. Another way to get the name of the decision maker is simply to call the company and ask, "What is the name of the (manager, owner, foreman, department head of ___, VP of __?) Would you spell it for me, please?"

Once you have the target name, talk to your network again and ask if they know this person, or possibly someone else who knows this person. Tell the contact who knows the decision maker that you wish to set up an interview with this person, and ask if they will call in advance for you so the decision maker will know who you are when you call. If the connecting contact person is new, you must go though your whole routine to gain her confidence—enthusiastically explain what you want to do and why you're a top candidate for that work.

If you cannot get a contact to call in advance for you, call or write to the decision maker directly. Mention the name of your referral immediately, then use your thirty-second commercial. (See *Set Up an Interview with a Phone Call*, p. 131, and *Construct a Winning Cover Letter*, p. 73.)

*Chapter Five*

*Marketing Savvy*

## *Don't Wait for Job Openings.*

Don't wait for job openings—look for potential openings.

❦ A good example came from a client, Rachel, who was targeting a sales position. She researched companies and selected four to target with a highly personalized letter. The morning after mailing the letters, she received a phone call from a vice president who said, "I just read your letter and had to call you. We don't have any openings right now, but I'd feel like an idiot if I didn't interview you." She interviewed with the VP, and he offered her an excellent position, available in three months. Confidently, she continued her job search knowing she had this offer in her back pocket.

The employer knows about future openings before anyone else. Employees may have given early notice (going back to school, permanent pregnancy leave, or being promoted or transferred). Or the boss knows someone has a poor performance and won't make it past his warning or probation time. Companies or departments may be expanding or adding new products and services. All of these things the boss knows before anyone else and before taking action to fill the positions. The employer is thinking about who to hire and is very receptive to meeting candidates at this time.

When the time is within a few weeks of filling the position, the boss announces it to the company by telling his peers and employees, putting it in the company newsletter or on the bulletin board, and notifying the human resources department (if the company has such a department). The employer also tells his friends, spouse and neighbors. He is hoping to get a referral or possibly promote or transfer someone to fill the position. Referrals are rated very high with employers because the recommendation comes from *someone they know and it is so much easier to hire this way*. No expense, no frustrating hours of pouring over resumes, no agonizing interviews with unqualified people.

About eighty percent of all jobs are filled by word-of-mouth by the time they reach this point. Another aspect to consider is that employers often can and do create new positions when they meet someone they want on board.

If the employer still cannot fill the position any other way, then it's time to advertise—the last resort.

# Use the Most Successful Job Search Methods.

No matter what state the economy is in, no matter how high or low unemployment is, there are always good jobs available. It's just as frustrating for employers to find good employees as it is for you to find a good job. It's just a matter of *finding* the job openings and potential job openings. And that depends on the kinds of job search methods you use. The two most successful job search methods, in order, are:

1. Finding a job through networking.
2. Finding a job by applying to the employer directly.

About eighty percent of all jobs are filled by word-of-mouth, or by networking with your friends, relatives, and acquaintances. One person tells another, and that person tells another, and so forth. As discussed in the networking section, the more eyes and ears you have in the job market looking for job leads for you, the greater your chances of finding your dream job.

The second best method is to apply to employers directly. That means you go right up to the place of business, walk in the door and ask for a manager, supervisor, owner, department head, big cheese, or top dog (just kidding), and tell them why you're interested in their company and what you can do for their company. Sometimes you may have to fill out an application or leave your resume and make contact later by phone or make an appointment to see the employer. (See also *Apply Directly to Employers in Person*, p. 133.)

If you use these two methods as your primary ways of searching for a job, you increase your chances dramatically.

# The More Methods You Use, the Faster You Will Find a Job.

Networking and applying to employers directly in person are the two most successful ways to find a job. Using a combination of methods increases your chances even more. Studies show that job seekers who find work in the least amount of time use a combination of job search methods. However, job seekers who used *more* than four methods became less effective.

The trick is not to make yourself crazy trying to do everything. Pick one or two additional methods that you think will work for your situation. Make sure that networking and applying directly to employers are your primary methods—where you spend the majority of your time and energy.

Other job search methods you should consider are: applying directly to employers using a personalized letter or a phone call, using the want ads, using a recruiter, employment agency or your school's placement firm, and using the internet. All of these methods are described in this book.

Of course, the job search methods you choose won't help much if you haven't gone to the trouble of identifying what kind of work you'd love to do and why you're qualified to do it. That is the essential foundation on which your job search is built.

# *Be Politely Persistent.*

One-third of job hunters give up too soon. They abandon their job search before finding their target job and either stop looking altogether or accept a menial job. This dismal situation can be avoided by simply being more persistent. Churchill's quote, "Never, NEVER give up," is very appropriate to the job search.

Usually people get discouraged and frustrated because of one or more of the following: 1) they are not targeting the work they love, 2) they haven't determined why they perform this job well, 3) they haven't networked continually with a clear message about their target work and skills, 4) they haven't thoroughly researched companies that do their target work, 5) they haven't been using a combination of job search methods, which include networking and applying to employers directly, 6) they haven't studied and practiced effective interviewing techniques, 7) they haven't spent, at the very least, thirty hours per week on their job search.

Your job search will take you longer than you think—it does for everyone. Those few "lucky" people who find a job magically in a short period of time usually have a strong network already in place, know what they want, and work diligently to get it. They're not lucky, they're prepared, and they don't give up—not even for a day.

❧ The most persistent job seeker I know is Bob, whose target job was a body shop manager for a large car dealer. He called on a Friday afternoon. He had been laid off that morning, already had an interview set up for Monday, and needed a resume, pronto. He wasted no time whatsoever. In the next *two weeks*, he was a flurry of activity—and landed three interviews and two job offers. He found leads from insurance agents in the auto business. He visited car dealers and simply walked around the lots to get the "feel" of it. He overheard two salespeople talking about the shoddy work done in the body shop and their customers' complaints. That was all Bob needed. He fired off a letter to the general manager and was invited in for an interview. They wanted a proposal of what he would do if he had the job. They liked his proposal and promptly replaced the manager with him.

# *Plan Your Day and Your Week.*

Get up every morning, dress, and prepare for your new job of finding a job. Determine what goals you want to achieve each week, and write them out: I want to make __ calls, write __ letters, meet with __ people, make a list of __ target companies, research __ companies, and have __ interviews.

Every Sunday night, take out your planner or organizer, and plan your week. Set aside time to make phone calls, research at the library, and visit employers. Obviously, you will have to be flexible to accommodate face-to-face meetings and interviews, but fill in your time so you have definite tasks to perform, and stick to your plan. Your time will look something like this:

*Monday morning: Answer the Sunday want ads.*

*Monday afternoon: Visit a recruiter, employment agency, or job placement firm (if you deem it necessary to use this method).*

*Tuesday morning: Research at the library (information about target work, names of companies that do this work).*

*Tuesday afternoon: Call ten to twenty friends and relatives in my network, tell them what I want to do and ask for referrals.*

*Tuesday evening: Call anyone I couldn't reach during the day.*

*Wednesday morning: Research in the library.*

*Wednesday afternoon: Call more networking contacts and referrals. Write thank-you notes to everyone who helped me.*

*Thursday morning: Meet with two contacts, write two letters.*

*Thursday afternoon: Research on the internet, make more calls, write thank-you notes.*

*Friday morning: Visit three target employers.*

*Friday afternoon: Meet with two contacts, write thank-you notes.*

Planning your days and week, plus continuing in a proactive manner will not only keep your spirits up, but will help you find a job faster because you'll be busy, more organized, and productive.

# Find Potential Employers in the Phone Book.

Open the yellow pages to the industry or industries you are interested in, and make a list of the companies, phone numbers, and addresses. If you're not sure of the industry, look in the index for ideas or simply page through the entire yellow pages. You may discover new industries related to your target work.

To be thorough, drive by or visit each one, and go the library to research any articles about the businesses. You can also call the companies and ask for any literature they have available—a catalog, brochure, or sales information. Just say you're researching companies in that field for a project, if asked. When networking, ask your contacts what they know about these companies and if they know someone who works there.

If you're targeting work long distance, a large library will have yellow pages from major U.S. cities. Business phone numbers and addresses, nationwide, are available on CD-ROM and on the internet and can be accessed by industry.

Choose which way you want to approach these companies, or use a combination of methods: by telephone, in person, by a personalized letter, or through a contact.

## *Target Small Businesses.*

Two-thirds of all job openings are in companies with fewer than one hundred employees. You will find a job faster if you seek out small businesses, especially those with fewer than twenty employees or fewer than fifty employees. Who are they, and how do you find them? You find them by looking through the yellow pages, by going to the library and researching directories and periodicals, by asking your contacts, by obtaining membership lists of industry associations and the chamber of commerce, and by driving around.

Small companies are also much easier to approach. There are no human resource or personnel departments to hold you back. It's much easier to get in and see the boss. Small businesses are growing and hiring—that's where the jobs are.

One disadvantage is that small firms offer fewer benefits, such as health care. However, the far greater advantage is this: if you work in a prospering, growing business with fewer than twenty employees, you can ride its wave to success. As the small company grows and prospers, so will you. You'll have more varied responsibilities and wear more hats, because that is the nature of a small business.

❦ Consider Dennis, who went to work for a small electronics firm. At the time he was hired, they had seven employees who worked out of small, cramped offices. He had to perform two or three different jobs, but so did everyone. It was exciting, building the company, flying by the seat of his pants. After two years, the company built a fifty thousand square-foot office/warehouse and had thirty employees. In two more years, the firm doubled its office space by adding an identical building and the number of employees tripled. Today, after ten years, another forty thousand square-foot building has been added to accommodate three hundred employees, plus two hundred sales-people positioned globally. Dennis is enjoying the fruits of his labor as one of the top executives of this prosperous company.

# *Set Up an Interview with a Phone Call.*

Before making that oh-so-important phone call, make sure you know these things: what kind of work you're targeting, your top qualifications for the job, and why the employer should hire you. The more you know about the company, the greater your chances of gaining an interview. (See *Know the Company*, p. 161.)

Next, find out the name of the boss who would hire you. Get this information from your contacts, or research, or call the company. Always call the company anyway to verify the name, title, and spelling especially if your information is old, as from a directory.

When you make the call, having a referral helps tremendously (work those contacts!). If you don't have a referral, you might mention an article or information about their company such as an expansion, new products, their marketing techniques, etc., to show that you know something about their company. Then launch into your thirty-second commercial (See *Create a Thirty-Second Commercial*, p. 87.) explaining briefly what work you're seeking and a couple of your top skills or qualifications for it. Then ask for a meeting.

"I'd like to meet with you in the next day or two. Which day is best for you?"

"We don't have any openings right now."

"I understand. I would still like to meet with you in case you have an opening in the future." Remember, you are looking for potential openings, not just openings. If they still say no, try one more time.

"Then I'd like to talk to you about your business. I'm interested in knowing more so I can find a position. Perhaps you can advise me, or tell me the names of others who may be interested in my skills. What do you say?"

Being politely persistent is desirable. Pushy is not.

Follow up with a handwritten thank-you note with your networking card enclosed, even if you didn't meet with the contact. They could have an opening the following week or refer you to others. If you meet with him, an after-interview business letter should be sent.

# *Apply Directly to Employers in Person.*

Applying to employers in person is the second most successful job method you can use. If you are a blue collar worker, this method is the number one most successful method for you. It works especially well in small companies, where there is no personnel or human resource department to screen you out. The boss is easier to identify and approach, and small companies are where the job growth is happening.

Before you walk through those doors, prepare by finding out as much as you can about the company. Visit it beforehand if possible, talk to your contacts, and conduct research at the library. If you can't find much on the company, at least know the industry well, who its competitors are, and how you will help the business. Also, have your resume ready and possibly a personalized cover letter to leave in case you don't gain a meeting. Call ahead and ask what the boss's name is along with title and spelling.

Be well groomed and dressed appropriately, then walk in and ask for the boss by name. If asked, explain that you're looking for work by using your thirty-second commercial. If the boss can't meet with you right then, try to make an appointment. If that fails, leave your resume and cover letter and fill out an application if one is required. The next day, follow up with a phone call, and call back each day until you can talk to the boss. When you get the boss on the line, use your thirty-second commercial and try to make an appointment regardless of whether the company has any job openings. This method works well in small companies.

❧ Robert was searching for a job as a salesperson in a title company. He went on vacation to the city he wanted to move to, rented a car, and drove around downtown. He came to a large, tall building with smoked glass and chrome entry complete with a fountain. He was impressed with the building and figured the company must be successful. He walked in, asked for the vice president of sales, and was granted a meeting. He hit if off with the VP and was given a tour and met more people. Robert was hired on the spot and started work in two weeks, complete with an excellent salary-plus-commission package and a company car.

# *Get the Most Out of Want Ads.*

Your chances of getting a job through the want ads are roughly one in ten—not very good odds, but worth a shot just to cover all the bases. The want ads can be helpful for discovering new companies in your field and exploring wages, job requirements, and job descriptions. The first rule of thumb is to the read the want ads cover to cover. Make notes of companies in your field, salaries, or possible job targets you'd like to research more.

Check out trade magazines for want ads in your specific field. You may have to subscribe to them if they are not at your library. The *National Business Employment Weekly* is available at the library and lists the weekly ads from all regional editions of the *Wall Street Journal,* plus carries excellent job search articles.

Go to the library, and try to find information about the company. (See *Use the Library for Job Leads and Research,* p. 143.) When writing your letter, mention some tidbit of information you've uncovered in your research to make your letter stand out. Show how closely your qualifications match the qualifications mentioned in the ad. If yours are mismatched to theirs, skip that ad. You don't need to waste time pursuing pie-in-the-sky jobs. Keep your letter brief, and ask for a meeting at the end (See *Construct a Winning Cover Letter*, p. 73.)

What if they ask for salary history or salary requirements? You can be eliminated at this point for naming figures too high or two low. (See *Don't Mention Salary in a Resume or Cover Letter*, p. 75.)

Want ads generate a rush of responses two to four days after the ad is placed. Hand deliver your letter Monday morning to get a jump start, or wait a few days to mail it, so it's viewed after the rush with fewer competitors. If possible, call the company a few days after receipt of your letter and ask for a meeting.

Blind ads—ads that don't mention the name of the company—are particularly unrewarding. It could be an unstable company, an employment agency or recruiter padding their resume banks, or your current employer!

# *Use a Recruiter or Employment Agency.*

Using recruiters is a favored job search method of executives and professionals. And quite a few companies use recruiters. However, you are still competing with a large number of rivals. The recruiter's job, and employment agencies, is to fill the position for the employer, not to find you, the job hunter, a job. Your chances are far greater to land a good job by researching companies, networking, and approaching the companies on your own.

The employment agency's and the recruiter's fees are paid by the employer. The employer can save a great deal of money by hiring you directly. Perhaps you can negotiate the saved fee as part of your salary (the fee is typically fifteen to twenty percent of the annual salary). It's a good idea to use a recruiter or employment agency—but as a secondary job search method.

Recruiters and employment agencies generally want top candidates who have a solid background in a specific field, not career changers or people just starting a career. Recruiters also approach peak performers who are currently employed, who otherwise wouldn't be your competition.

Recruiters and employment agencies can provide job leads you may not find otherwise, tell you what salary to expect, and pre-screen you for the open position. The rest of the legwork is up to you—research the company, map out your unique selling position for that specific company, and conduct a stimulating interview.

The best way to find a recruiter for your specific industry is to ask people in your field. They may have been contacted by a recruiter or use recruiters in their business. The library has a directory called *The Directory of Executive Recruiters*, which is organized by industry, function, and location. Write a strong cover letter, with resume, to the targeted recruiter(s) and specify what you are looking for, your credentials, your salary range, and if you're willing to relocate. As always during your job search, focus on what you have to offer, not what you want. Do not call the recruiter, they will call you if they have a position that fits your background. To contact an employment agency, write, visit in person, or call.

# *Surf the Internet for Leads and Research.*

If you have a computer and a modem, you can surf the internet for job leads, make new contacts, research companies, apply for jobs, and post your resume on the net. If you don't have a computer and modem or feel uncomfortable navigating your way though the internet, visit a large library, and ask the librarian to help you. She may perform the search for you or show you how to do it. Using the internet is fast and timely, but can be costly and time consuming. The best way to use the internet is for research and making contacts through chat rooms. High tech jobs are more likely to be listed on the internet than non-technical jobs, but remember that the number one most successful way to land a job is through networking, and second is applying to the employer in person. Nothing beats meeting a person face-to-face.

E-mail is a very helpful tool for sending and receiving messages, especially long distance. You can also send cover letters and resumes via e-mail, avoiding the post office altogether. To use your e-mail address in the job search, it should be politically correct. You don't want to print an e-mail address like "hotlovin" on your resume. Print your e-mail address on your networking card, letters, and all correspondence, and collect e-mail addresses from your contacts and potential employers.

The internet is a wonderful place to unearth information about companies in your field. Large corporations are easy to find, but many smaller companies have web sites, too. If you can't find a specific company by searching, simply call the company and ask if they have a web site you can visit.

See the following section for job search web site addresses.

# *Visit Job Search Resource Sites on the Internet.*

The following is a list of the best of the web sites for job search.

## Job Search Resources

*About Work*  http://www.aboutwork.com

Includes networking, a self-assessment test, expert advice, a list of top ten sites online, interviewing tips, and more.

*America's Employers*  http://www.americasemployers.com/

Includes open jobs, chat room, resume bank, networking information, company databases, recruiters, and more.

*Career Mosaic*  http://www.careermosaic.com/cm/

Lists openings from major companies and a "jobs.offered" index with more than 22,000 postings sorted daily from international newsgroups .

*The Monster Board*  http://www.monster.com/

Employer profiles for more than four thousand companies and more than five thousand job listings, and fifty thousand worldwide.

*Online Career Center*  http://www.occ.com

One of the largest online job search resources, with a database of jobs searchable by type, location, etc. Also features a resume posting, career assistance, career fairs, a college recruiting forum, and more.

## Job Listings

*America's Job Bank*  http://www.ajb.dni.us/index.html

Includes approximately one hundred thousand private sector and government job listings.

*Career Path*  http://www.ajb.dni.us/

Job listings, research, job search tips, career resources.

*JobBank USA MetaSearch*  http://www.jobbankusa.com/search.html

## Post Your Resume

*World Wide Web Employment Office*

http://www.harbornet.com/biz/office/annex.html

Lists resumes by field and occupation.

*Tripod*  http://www.tripod.com/work/resume/linklist.html

Lists sites to post your resume. Can keep your identity secret until the employer pays a small fee.

## Contacts

http://www.idealist.org  Organizations, programs, and services.

http://www.switchboard.com/ People, companies, and websites.

# Use the Library for Leads and Research.

Research is the foundation of a good job search. You can uncover job leads, discover new companies in your field, research targeted companies, and more. To make a strong impression, it is especially helpful to gather background information before an interview. Research does not replace networking, but adds value to it.

The library you choose should be the largest library in your city. Generally, it will have the most information. Plan to spend several hours at the library, once a week.

The first order of business is to put together a list of potential employers. You may have one started from your networking activities. Visit the librarian in the reference section, and tell her specifically what kind of work you are seeking and the industries involved. She will tell you the best directories to use for your situation out of the hundreds available. A good place to begin is with *Directories in Print*, which will provide a description of all the directories available.

Once you've located several directories, browse through them to become familiar with them and to see if they will fit your situation. Make a list of the companies that match your industry, location, and the size of company you're seeking. Most general directories will not provide much more than name, address, phone number, size, and name of CEO. Smaller companies may not be listed at all. When you are ready to contact these companies, always verify names and addresses by calling the company, as directories tend to be dated.

Check out the *Job Hunter's Sourcebook*. It will show you where to find job leads and other job search resources, according to your industry. Another source is *Dun's Career Guide,* which lists employers, hiring areas, contact names, etc.

The next step is to find more detailed information about your targeted employers through articles in periodicals. This will also uncover more leads to smaller companies.

# *Get the Most From Periodicals.*

Researching periodicals will provide information about industry trends, potential job leads, specific topics, and specific companies. Look for promotions, growth, new products, start-ups, relocations, buy-outs, and mergers. All are clues to potential job openings.

General business magazines include *Barron's, Business Week, Forbes, Fortune,* and *Inc. Magazine.* Newspapers include the *Wall Street Journal, The New York Times, The Business Journal,* and your local newspapers, or the newspaper of the city where you are relocating. (You may have to subscribe to the last one.)

The best periodical to study is the *National Business Employment Weekly,* published weekly, exclusively for job seekers. Each issue compiles want ads from all the regional editions of the *Wall Street Journal* and offers a variety of excellent articles about every aspect of the job search.

You can search for specific companies or specific topics in articles on microfilm or CD-ROM. Check with your reference librarian to see which publications are available at your library.

Trade publications often have industry information, want ads, and names of companies you can't find anywhere else. When networking with someone in your targeted field, ask them what publications they read. Look up trade publications in the *Standard Rate & Data Service Business Publications Directory* and the *Gale Directory of Publications and Broadcast Media*. One challenge is that your library may not have copies of trade publications. Call the publisher and ask for a sample, or buy a sample. If it fits your targeted job, subscribe to it.

Make notes or copies of articles of interest to you, and keep them in your files at home. (See *Keep Files of Prospective Employers*, p. 157.) Mentioning an article in a conversation or letter is a good opener.

# *Break Through to the Decision Maker.*

There are five ways to set up an interview: referral, cover letter, phone call, applying in person, and the internet, as we have covered. Still, no matter how brilliantly you write your letter or conduct your phone conversation, it may be difficult to actually speak to the boss who has the power to hire you. Try these additional tips to reach that very important person:

Call before 8 a.m., at lunch time, and after 5 p.m. Usually the assistant is gone at this time, and chances are the boss will answer the phone.

Don't leave a message on voice mail. Try calling at different times of the day. If that doesn't work, leave a short, upbeat message naming your referral (if you have one) and explain what kind of work you are looking for and that you'd like to meet. Leave your phone number, but state you will call back. Keep trying.

Ask when the boss will be in, and make an appointment to call then.

Ask the assistant for help. "I'm in the job market for a
_____. I'd really like to discuss employment opportunities with
Ms. Williams. Can you help me?"

Call the CEO's office and get referred from his assistant to
another office by telling her what kind of work you're seeking and
asking her to recommend the person to call. Then call your targeted
person and open with, "I was referred to you from Mr. Gates office..."

Fax a short letter to the boss similar to your cover letter. Focus on what you can do for the company, and ask for a meeting.

Send a short note by e-mail similar to the above letter. Cour-
teously ask the assistant for the address.

Be politely persistent. Call or make contact every couple of
days, or once a week for executives, until you reach the boss. You
have nothing to lose if he is not returning your call anyway, but
always be respectful and gracious. You don't want to burn bridges!

If none of these techniques work, wait a month, and if you're
still in the job market, start over by mailing your letter and resume as
if you had never made contact before.

# *Your Job Search Reflects the Way You Perform Your Work.*

Your job search is a job. Employers notice how you handle yourself and the tasks that come along with the job search. Everything you do gives the employer a glimpse of how you will perform on the job. If your written materials are sloppy, you probably are, too. If they are well thought out and organized, obviously you have planned and taken the time to organize—just as you will perform your work. If you say you will call at a specific time and don't, or make an appointment and reschedule, will you treat customers like that, too? If you researched the company, you are a thorough person. If you give up after one call, you don't try very hard on the job. If you perform something as important as your job search in a slipshod way, the message to the employer is that you really don't care. Why would he hire people like that?

Every contact you make with the employer is of the utmost importance and should be approached in the best manner possible. That includes phone calls, letters, dropping in to pick up an application, e-mail, faxes, or any contact at all. Don't slack off with receptionists or assistants—they often share their opinions with the boss, and the boss listens. Put a lot of thought and care into your presentations. Take the extra time to proofread your written materials, and have another person who is good at that sort of thing do it, too. Practice your phone conversations with a friend. Stand up and smile when speaking on the phone—you'll sound more energetic. Role play the interview with a friend and answer tough questions. Do as much research as you can, and use it in your presentations. Dress for success in all meetings and whenever you leave the house, in case you run into an important contact.

# *Manage Your Job Search Time Wisely.*

In addition to making your job search a full time job, managing your time effectively will reap rewards faster. It's only logical to spend the majority of your time on the most successful job search methods. Those methods are 1) networking, and 2) applying to employers directly. Your chances of landing a job using one or both of these methods is roughly eighty percent. Therefore, you should spend eighty percent of your time using these methods. Research should also be counted in this time frame.

Of course, no one knows in advance where the job lead will come from that will land the job, so you want to cover all bases. Your chances are about one in ten, or ten percent, that you will find the job through the want ads, so spend ten percent of your time on want ads.

If you're using a recruiter or employment agency, your chances are also one in ten of finding a job that way, so spend ten percent of your time with these agencies. If you are searching for a job with salary ranges of $40,000 and above, and especially $70,000 and up, your chances are somewhat higher using a recruiter, providing you meet their guidelines. (See *Use a Recruiter or Employment Agency*, p. 137.)

The one wild card in the bunch is the internet. Because it is so new, data showing job search results using the internet are not available. If your job target is in the computer industry, the internet could work well for you, and you should spend a good portion of your job search time on the internet. But do *not* place less importance on networking and applying directly to employers. If your job target is not in the computer industry, limit your time searching on the internet to ten percent or less. *Do* conduct company research on the internet. (See *Surf the Internet for Leads and Research*, p. 139, and *Visit Job Search Research Sites on the Internet*, p.141.)

Plan your entire week on Sunday or Monday morning. List your goals for the week and each day. Make out a To Do list, and follow it every day. You will be more productive and boost your confidence, as well as land a better job faster.

# *Follow-Up on Job Leads Immediately.*

As soon as you hear about a job lead, go into action immediately. You don't want to miss out on an opportunity because you procrastinated about checking it out. Often people land jobs because they were in the right place at the right time. They walked in the day someone quit, or made the right phone call just when the boss got the go-ahead to add to her staff. Coincidence? Perhaps a small portion is, but you can increase your luck by being relentless and timely in checking out all job leads.

Depending on the level of the job and how desperate the employer is to fill it, it's possible to be hired on the spot. More than likely though, it will take two to four contacts before a job offer is tendered, or even before an interview is set up. All the more reason to follow up on job leads quickly—to begin the job hunter/employer courtship.

Job leads come from a multitude of sources: networking, library directories, magazine articles, newspaper articles, associations, clubs, the internet, want ads, etc. If the lead came from a source other than a person, the first step is to find someone who knows about the company or anyone who works there, by checking with your network. A referral is the best foot in the door you can have. Then, do research at the library, and figure out your approach. Write and/or call the targeted person at the company, mentioning your referral, article, industry gossip, or interesting information. By now you should know the drill—give them your thirty-second commercial, and ask for an interview.

# *Search for a Job Long Distance.*

Searching for a job long distance uses many of the same principles as a job search conducted in your home town. Planning, organization, and timing are key factors to make your long distance search successful and keep costs to a minimum.

First, define your preferred geological location by city, state, or area. Then identify the companies in that area that perform the work you're seeking. Or perhaps you have identified the companies first and have decided that you are willing to relocate to certain areas. Also, the corporate office may be located in a different state.

Research the targeted companies through library directories, periodicals, and the internet. Do not neglect your contacts. Many job seekers incorrectly assume that since they are moving to a far away city, their contacts can't help them. When networking, include your preferred location and ask if your contact knows anyone who lives in that city. Soon, you will be talking to or e-mailing someone in that far away city and will begin to build your network there. (See *Build A Network*, p. 95.)

To approach companies, call or write mentioning a referral, if possible, or some information you have learned from researching. The combination of calling and writing works well. After you have developed a rapport (and deem a visit is worthwhile) ask for a meeting. If you have a specific time planned to visit the city, set up your meetings then. If your time is more flexible, set up the first meeting, then approach other companies about visiting during that time.

Naturally, timing is everything, so do as much research and networking as possible before you contact the companies. Contact companies in the same time frame to try to meet with as many as possible when you visit the city, regardless of whether they have any current openings. Once you have met them face-to-face, it's easier to continue the courtship long distance.

The employer may be concerned that you will change your mind about relocating. Convince him that you are committed to moving. Some job hunters use a friend's address and phone number that live in the area in order to use a local address, or they plan an extended stay and conduct their job search from the targeted city.

# *Keep Files of Prospective Employers.*

It is crucial that you stay on top of things and make that important phone call at the right time, send those thank-you notes and letters at the right time, and know exactly where you stand with each employer you contact.

The best filing system is to set up 8½ x 11-inch manila folders to store all the articles, printed internet information, copies from the library, and various notes you have gathered, arranged alphabetically by company. A plastic file box from the office supply store works great if you don't have a file cabinet or drawer. You can then access this information easily.

For an action file, use 3 x 5-inch index cards with a box to hold them. These cards will contain the employer's name, address, and phone. Use them to record all actions you have taken with the employer, including phone calls, letters, and thank-you notes, and what the results were. Record personal information such as the name of your contacts children, hobbies, home town, alma mater, etc. What is the assistant's name and what are her interests? Personal information can break the ice when you call or visit and help others to remember you in good terms.

Keep your top five or ten employer action cards in the front of your box, and when planning your day or week, review them to see what needs to be done. These are your hottest leads, your "A" group. Next is your "B" group, the warm leads, then "C" group, the new or cold leads. When things are slow, go through your B and C groups, and decide how to pursue—a new letter, a follow-up phone call, or an interesting article.

If you organize your files this way, you are prepared and ready at a moment's notice for a surprise telephone interview, a quickly composed letter, communication with contacts, or a last minute face-to-face interview.

# Chapter Six

# Ace the Interview

# *Know the Company.*

By now you're probably tired of hearing research, research, research. It's a proven fact that the more you know about the company, the greater your chances of winning a job offer, and of finding a company that will make you happy. How much money would you make per hour if you got this job? That's how much you are paying yourself for time spent on research. When you have an interview lined up, it is the time to really start digging.

Reach for the telephone, and call all your contacts. (Aren't you glad you've built a good network?) Ask if they know anything about the company you are interviewing with or anyone who works there, especially your interviewer. Continue gathering information until you have exhausted your contacts (not literally!).

At the library, look up the interviewer's name in *Who's Who*. You never know who may be there! If the interviewer is listed, incorporate that information in your networking. For instance, if you know your interviewer went to Colorado State University and is from

Chicago, ask your contacts if they know anyone who is from Chicago or went to Colorado State University. You'd be surprised at how often you'll find a match. How about opening the interview with, "I understand you went to school at CSU. Did you know a Doris Hillway? She remembers you quite fondly." Smiling, the employer says, "Oh my, yes. We had several classes together. Haven't thought of her in years."

At the library, comb though local periodicals, newspapers, and trade magazines with the help of your reference librarian. Information about a small company will be harder to find but not impossible. If you can't find much on the company, dig up as much as possible about the industry—trends, new products, the competition, the movers and shakers in the field.

You may not use all this information in your interview, but even one timely tidbit can set you apart from your rivals. You will be more informed and can answer questions well. You will ask the employer insightful questions and carry on a stimulating discussion. It will also boost your confidence and self-esteem.

In a nutshell: If you want the job, do the work.

# *Name Your Top Five Qualifications for the Job.*

Let's turn the table around for a minute and imagine that you are the employer. What skills, special knowledge, and characteristics would the perfect candidate for this job possess? Is special training, a license, or certificate necessary? Does this job require a degree or specific education? What personality traits would the perfect candidate have?

Make a list of these qualifications from the employer's view. Draw a line down the middle of the page and on the right side list your qualifications. Match as many of the employer's qualifications as possible.

What experience do you have that is relevant? What skills did you use when performing this work? Think back about your education, training, and any seminars or classes you have attended. Which are relevant to this job? What special knowledge, insight, or information do you possess that would be an asset to this job? Some examples are:

business contacts, language(s), inside knowledge of competitors and their products, familiarity with a territory, thorough understanding of a specialized process or technique, etc.

And finally we come to characteristics. Did you know that ATTITUDE is the number one trait employers look for when hiring? Just what kind of attitude they are looking for will depend on the employer and the job. Think very carefully about what the employer would like to see and how your personality traits match it. Obviously, the personality traits of a public relations person will be different than those of a computer programmer. All employers want a positive, enthusiastic, can-do attitude and a person who will fit in with the company.

After you have made a list of your top qualifications, you must illustrate your skills and characteristics with examples of how you have used them in the past. Think of accomplishments that demonstrate your skills and personality. It's not enough to say, "I work well with people." To make your point, tell a short work-related story that shows how you solved a problem or met a challenge using that particular skill. The stories are "proof" of your skills. Have them ready to go for your interview.

# Why Should the Employer Hire You?

Each and every person has a special and unique combination of skills, knowledge, experience, and personality traits that no one else has. The trick is to present your particular package to the employer and show her how you can perform this work like no one else. This is sometimes referred to as your "unique selling position."

What makes you different/better than the ten other people applying for the job? Again, the more you know about the company, the better you can answer this question. What are the challenges/problems facing the company or department now and in the near future? How can your special skills, knowledge, and experience help solve this challenge? That is your unique selling position. What is the company's philosophy or mission statement? How do you fit in?

You can uncover the challenges and problems facing the company and its philosophy through thorough investigation. That means digging for information by networking, informational interviewing, and research.

When you practice the interview, answer the employer's question, "Why should I hire you?" Please note that answers like, "Because I'm the best candidate for the job," or "I won't let you down," are unacceptable. You need to explain in detail WHY.

# *Role Play the Interview.*

Most of us don't go to interviews very often, so we tend to get rusty. The more practice you have, the more confident you will be at crunch time.

Make up a list of questions you think the employer is likely to ask you, then add some zingers. You need to be prepared for unexpected and difficult questions. What questions do you fear or make you uncomfortable? Can you answer these:

"Have you ever been fired or asked to resign?"

"Why do you have these gaps between jobs?"

"Why did you leave this company?"

"You seem to be over/under qualified for this position."

"You've had quite a few jobs recently."

"Have you ever disagreed with your boss?"

"What would your previous employer say about you?"

"Why are you changing careers?"

"Why should I hire you?"

Whatever topic makes you uncomfortable needs to be brought out in the open and dealt with in the best way. You may not be asked that dark question, but you should be prepared for it.

Have a friend role play the interviewer and ask you questions. Sometimes it helps to sit in two chairs back-to-back so you can maintain a level of seriousness. Practice answering questions with short work stories illustrating your skills and accomplishments. Strategize how to answer the tough questions. Practice a summary for the end, questions for the interviewer, and negotiating your salary.

Another method is to use a tape recorder, or video recorder while role playing, then play it back and listen as if you were the employer.

# *Practice Interviews With Companies Lowest on Your Target List.*

The best way to practice an interview is in a real interview. Instead of beginning with your top targets first, start at the bottom of your list of potential employers. Or pick one or two in which you're not interested, and line up interviews with them.

This way, you can practice phone calls, see the response to your letters and resume, and rehearse a real, live interview. See first-hand how your research pays off. If you don't get the job offer, who cares? And if you do, well, being able to turn down an offer boosts your self-confidence. Informational interviewing also provides good practice for the real interview.

❦ A woman named Michelle tried this method of practice interviewing with a company that was too small and new for her purposes. She met with the owner who was very impressed by her and offered her a job. She politely declined, stating that she was just beginning her job search and wanted to see what else was available before she made a decision. The owner called her every week for three weeks and asked if she would accept the job, adding a little more incentive each time. She still did not want the job, but she was so flattered that he aggressively pursued her, and knowing she had a job offer in her back pocket rocketed her self-esteem. She turned down another offer that wasn't exactly right and finally found the job of her dreams—all within three weeks.

## *Dress for Success, Not a Date.*

Is what you wear to an interview really that important? Absolutely, definitely, YES. You only have one chance to make a good first impression. The employer will size you up in the first few minutes, and your clothes are a big portion of that impression.

What should you wear to an interview? There is no cut and dried rule that will fit all job interviews. Obviously, a banker will dress differently than a construction worker. The common denominator for all job interviews is to dress appropriately for that position. Dress as if you were going to an important meeting as an employee in that company, or dress as your new boss would dress. If you have time, go by the place of work ahead of time and observe what the employees are wearing. Just be sure it's not casual day you're observing!

Generally, most people wear a business suit or dress. If you don't have the appropriate quality clothing, it is well worth investing in an interview outfit or two. Choose quality fabrics, conservative colors and styles, and subtle prints. Wear good shoes the same color or darker than your outfit. Women must wear hose, but avoid dark stockings with a light colored outfit. Men's socks should match the pants or shoes. Go easy on the jewelry, after shave, and perfume. This is an interview, not a date. Your hair should be freshly styled and nails clean and manicured. Avoid anything outlandish or eccentric. Remember that you want to blend into the company, not stand out like a peacock.

Carry a good quality purse or briefcase. A leather notebook is a good way to carry a note pad, extra resumes, and your reference list. If it is appropriate to take samples of your work, make sure they are organized and well presented in a good quality carrying case.

# *Treat Employers With Respect, but as Equals.*

You do not want to look down on your interviewer or put the interviewer on a pedestal. The interviewer, or employer, should be treated with respect, but as your equal.

Saying it and doing are two different things, especially if you are in awe of the employer. To gain confidence before the meeting, review all the notes and research you have compiled about the company. Did you get the scoop on the interviewer himself? Review that, too. (See *Know the Company*, p. 161.)

On an index card, write out your five best qualifications and accomplishments that you want to bring up in the interview. On the back of the card, write out five thoughtful and insightful questions for the employer that will show your knowledge of the company and provide feedback that will help you make a decision about working there.

Remember that you have valuable skills, knowledge, and expertise to offer the company. You are offering value, not just filling a slot.

Do not in any way, shape, or form regard your interviewer with thinly veiled contempt or arrogance. No matter who your interviewer is—personnel or an assistant—he or she has something to offer you. If someone's personality grates on you, bury your contempt, and bury it deep. If the interviewer detects any breath of arrogance, you're history. Besides, if you think a job or company is beneath you, then why are you there?

## *Three Golden Questions You Must Answer Correctly.*

You may be thinking that there are hundreds of interview questions the employer can ask you, not to mention trick questions. How can you possibly prepare for that? Don't drive yourself crazy trying to analyze all the possible questions and answers that may arise during your interview.

No matter what questions the employer asks you, all of them boil down to three basic questions. They are:

1. What can you do for us?

2. Why did you choose this company?

3. Will you fit in?

The first one, "What can you do for us?" is answered with your skills and knowledge. "Proof" of these skills and knowledge is illustrated by examples from your past work experience (or volunteer work, life experiences, or projects in school). The examples should be in the form of accomplishments with results stated.

"Why did you choose this company?" is answered with specific insights and information you have gleaned from research and networking about that particular company. Every employer and company is unique, and each one prefers someone who recognizes and understands that uniqueness and can fill the bill. (See *Know the Company*, p 161.)

"Will you fit in?" With this question, the employer wants to know if you will get along and work well with your peers, the workers you supervise or lead, and the top brass. Do your personality, work ethics, and beliefs fit in with the rest of the team? This question is answered by everything you say and do. (See *Name Your Top Five Characteristics*, p. 17.)

The interviewer probably will not pose these questions directly. When asked a question during the interview, pause for a moment and think about which basic question it leads back to, then answer accordingly. It is your responsibility to make sure you have given the interviewer answers to these three questions, even if they were not referred to. The interviewer needs this information to make a decision about hiring you.

# *Answer Illegal Questions by Determining the Real Concern.*

By law, interviewers cannot ask you questions about marital status, age, race, ethnic origins, or religion. Larger companies tend to know the discrimination laws very well and will probably not ask a question on these taboo topics. However, it can happen with a less informed interviewer. What should you do?

First, recognize that the interviewer is probably not trying to discriminate against you, but is awkwardly trying to find out 1) can you perform the job? or 2) will you fit in with the company? He simply chose an ungainly way of asking the question. Your aim is to get a job offer, not start a lawsuit.

For instance, you may be asked (illegally), "Do you have children?" Perhaps the employer is worried about prolonged absence if your children are sick, or your ability to handle the traveling aspect of the job. The appropriate questions would be, "Are there any obstacles preventing you from traveling in this job?" or "We have a strict attendance policy here. Can you adhere to it?"

You can avoid the issue and answer the question at the same time by saying, "If you're worried whether I will miss work, my attendance is exemplary. Please check with my past employer." Or address the problem head-on. "Yes, I have two children. I have excellent child care and back-up care if they are ill. It will not interfere with my work." It is also possible the company has strong family values and the employer is asking because they desire employees with the same values.

If an off-limit topic comes up, try to figure out the "real" concern, and answer it. You can always point out that a question is illegal, but you run the risk of alienating your interviewer. If you genuinely feel you are being discriminated against, leave and go on to the next employer, unless you want to spend your time and money on a lawsuit.

# The Interview Is a Stimulating, Two-Way Conversation.

The typical, average interview goes like this: You meet, the employer says, "Tell me a little about yourself," and then asks inadequate questions about your work experience. He then explains a little about the position he has open and asks if you have any questions. That signals the end of the interview.

No wonder it's difficult for employers and job hunters to find a decent match! Many employers don't have much interview experience except from when *they* were looking for work, and now they use the same scenario. Job hunters usually don't have much experience either, since we will do practically anything to avoid the whole process.

Think of your interview as a meeting. In a meeting, you both participate equally, sharing ideas—a two-way stimulating conversation. You speak half of the time and the interviewer speaks half of the time.

Want to get a jump start? You ask the first question, using your inside knowledge of the company. Try, "I met with Marty Shriver from sales last week, and he told me a little about your new product, _____. That must be exciting for you. When do you plan to have it on-line?" or "I read an article last week in *The Business Journal* that (use the company name) has experienced record growth and plans to add a third location. When do you anticipate that will happen?"

The interviewer will know right up front that you are not the Average Joe, and the interview will take on a whole new, positive light. And you will be basking in it. Discussing the company early on gives you valuable insight in how to tailor your approach. Having a discussion rather than a question and answer period is powerful and puts you in the driver's seat as a resource, rather than an applicant. It also allows *you* to learn more, so you can decide if you want to work there.

# Don't Wait Until the End of the Interview to Ask Questions.

Another way to change the interview from a question and answer period into a two-way conversation is to ask questions throughout the interview, not just at the end. This technique is desirable because the more you learn about the company and position early on, the better you can tailor your answers to fit its needs.

Here's how to do it:

Employer: "Your resume states you cut costs by eighteen percent in your department last year. Tell me about that."

Job hunter: "I called a strategizing meeting with the eight people in my department, explaining that we needed to cut our costs without compromising our work. I let them set the goal, which incidentally, was five percent higher than I anticipated. We planned how to do it, how each person could contribute. It worked well. We achieved our goal in six months. I believe strongly in the teamwork concept, and I know (name of interviewing company) does, too. How has it been working in this department?"

Here's another example:

Employer: "How would your last boss describe you?"

Job hunter, without hesitation: "She would say I'm professional, dependable, perform my work well, and excel in customer service. That's why I won Employee of the Month four times last year. Are these the kind of qualities you're looking for?"

Asking a question at the end of your question will help you learn more along the way about the job and where you stand. Getting the interviewer to visualize you in the new position is a gold-medal technique. Here are more questions for the interviewer:

Would you describe the position for me?

Why is this position open?

If I had this job, what results would you like to see me produce?

Describe the people I would work with.

What's the greatest challenge facing your staff?

What are your goals for the upcoming year(s)?

Save questions about salary, vacation, and benefits until after a job offer has been tendered or *strong* hiring interest is shown.

# The Employer Considers Two Things—
# Abilities and Attitude.

An interesting concept developed at a seminar I attended. The seminar was geared for career counselors, human resource people, and anyone who worked with job hunters. Just before lunch, the instructor gave us an assignment (approximately sixty people). During our ninety minute lunch, we were to walk into a business, or call one, and ask the manager what was the number one quality he or she looked for when hiring. When we compared notes back at the seminar, we discovered an astounding majority of the employers said **attitude** was the number one attribute they looked for. Not training, not skills, not education, but attitude. Also, in a recent survey, eighty percent of employers said attitude was the number one quality they wanted. *Many employers commented that employees could be trained, but their attitude couldn't be changed.* Never forget this during your interviews.

What is the right attitude? It will be different for each employer and each job. Observe your interviewer closely, and try to match her demeanor, but don't force it. It's important to be yourself. Basically, all employers want a positive, enthusiastic, employee with a can-do attitude who works well with other employees.

Of course, the second attribute employers look for is your abilities, or potential abilities if training is involved. Can you perform the job? How well can you perform the job? Be prepared to communicate your abilities and skills as they relate to the new job to convince the employer you are the top candidate for the position. (*See Name Your Top Five Qualifications for the Job*, p. 163.)

# *How to Handle a Group Interview.*

There are several kinds of group interviews. The most common is a single applicant being interviewed by a panel of interviewers. Variations on the group interview include several applicants being interviewed at the same time and multiple back-to-back, one-on-one interviews, which sometimes last all day.

In any group situation, keep in mind several points. Always bring extra copies of your resume—twice as many as you think you need, and give them to each person. The basic principles of interviewing are the same: listen closely to the interviewer, communicate clearly your top skills and qualities, and answer the question, "Why should this company hire me?" The fact that the company uses group interviews shows they place a high value on teamwork. Make every effort to show you are a team player.

In the case of the single applicant being interviewed by a panel, try to identify the decision maker early on. He or she may be the quietest one there and not ask you a single question. The decision maker is the person you most want to monitor, but do not ignore anyone present. Address the person who asked the question, and acknowledge everyone during the answer. Be sure to ask questions as you go along—don't accept this as a grilling session. Ask what qualities they are seeking in the person to fill the job. The answers will show if they agree and what concerns each person has. For salary issues, see *Negotiate for Top Dollars*, p. 201. It is to your advantage to get them to name a figure first, or wait until you meet with the single decision maker to talk money.

During a day filled with multiple interviews with one company, you'll repeat yourself often, and that's fine. Ask each person questions to get different perspectives on the company and how it interacts. Try to stay fresh, but be yourself.

In the situation of several applicants being interviewed at once, often the applicants will be viewed as a "team" and given a "project" to act upon. The best way to handle this is to take charge immediately while being a team player. Acting as a mediator and asking others for their opinions (instead of spouting yours right away) will present you as a leader and give you an edge. Summarize the problem as the group sees it, and summarize the group's plan of action to the interviewing panel.

# *Testing. 1-2-3 Testing.*

More and more companies and government agencies are requiring testing of some kind. Many companies require certification for specific technical skills and training. A recent poll reported that twenty eight percent of large corporations screen applicants for drugs. Also popular are tests for personality, intelligence, aptitude, honesty, and handwriting analysis. You can refuse to take a test, or get the certification, but you will probably be out of the running if you do.

Certification and training for specific technical skills are often provided by the manufacturer of the product or service. An aptitude, or assessment test, given by the employer, tests for specific skills. It helps to brush up on skills such as keyboarding, mathematics, or whatever skills the job requires.

Personality tests show if you have the right personality for a specific job. Don't try to fake the answers or answer as you think they want you to. Just be yourself; if you don't get the job based on a test, you probably don't want that job.

If you are required to take a drug test, (usually a urine test), do not take cough syrup, drink gin, or eat poppy seeds before the test. In some tests, these foods show up as illegal drugs.

Handwriting analysis, personality tests, drug tests. Whatever test you come across, basically take it or forget about that job. There are many more jobs out there, particularly with small companies who usually don't require testing.

# Be Prepared to Steer the Interview Back on Track.

Chances are more likely that you will have an ill-prepared interviewer than a tough one. Many decision makers simply don't interview often and are not trained in the art of interviewing. Some decision makers fancy themselves as a "good judge of character" and rely on it. Others are simply inept, rude, chatter endlessly, or try to test you. Skilled interviewers are tough because they're prepared and adept at probing and prodding.

Whichever type of interviewer you face, it's up to you, the job hunter, to insure that the interviewer gets all the information he needs to make an informed decision about hiring you—your skills, accomplishments, and what you can do for the company. It is also your responsibility to gather all the information you need to make an informed decision about whether *you* want to work there.

Always be yourself. If you honestly don't know the answer, say so, don't try to wing it. Keep your patience in check, and bring the topic back to the new job parameters and how you can fill them. Ask questions. If your interviewer likes to talk, get him to talk about the job and the company. Before you leave, be sure to summarize what skills you bring to the table, and state your interest in the position.

# *Close the Sale.*

Closing the sale means leaving the best possible impression fresh in the interviewer's mind *and* finding out where you stand.

When the interviewer asks if you have any more questions, that is your signal that the end is near. If you haven't already done so, ask your prepared questions and any others that come to mind.

Now it's time for the close. The most effective method is to summarize what the job entails, how your qualifications match, and what you can do for the company. In short, describe why the employer should hire you and end with one of these closing lines:

"How do you think I would fit in with the group?"

"This has been an exciting meeting for me. This is a job I can perform well and contribute to your goals. What is the next step?"

"Here is a list of my references. Pat Milton at ABC can tell you more about that project we discussed. Do you need any more information?"

"When will you make a decision?"

"Shall we schedule another interview?"

"Is there anyone else I should meet before a decision is made?"

If possible, find out the general process and where you stand. Do they usually conduct multiple interviews? Interviews with others in the company? Who makes the final decision? When will it be made?

If you have decided you do not want the job, continue on as if you do. It is excellent practice for salary negotiation and knowledge of the company's pay scale. It's always possible to be referred to someone else or a different position. Besides, turning down a job offer will boost your ego.

Do not discuss salary until they have shown strong hiring interest or made an offer. If an offer is made, it is to your benefit to delay your final decision. (See *Negotiate for Top Dollars*, p. 201.)

# *Give the Employer a List of Your References After an Interview.*

Today many companies, especially large companies, want to avoid any incidents that might lead to a lawsuit regarding employees dismissals or their leaving the company. Typically, a potential employer wanting to do a background check on a candidate will only obtain name, rank, and serial number from past employers. Employers are afraid to give a former employee a bad reference, or admit a person is not eligible for rehire, for fear of a lawsuit. So they make it their policy not to say anything. This puts a damper on top performers.

The potential employer will think more highly of you if he can speak to a former boss or a business reference and glean information about your work performance and ethics. Even in a large company often there someone who is willing to bend the rules and speak to your potential employers as a reference. Line up your references, ask their permission, then type them on separate sheet of paper.

Employers are not interested in your references until they have met you and like what you have to offer. Do not mail or fax your references with your resume—the extra pages are just more unnecessary clutter at that point. After a good interview, hand the list of references to the interviewer. He will appreciate being able to contact your references easily and you will benefit knowing that you will receive glowing recommendations. It is another way to show your professionalism and organizational skills. (See *Line Up your References*, p. 91.)

If you have letters of recommendation, now is the time to give them to the interviewer. Mark the relevant sentences with a highlighter. These letters help, but not as much as a conversation with your references.

# *Make Notes After an Interview.*

Bring a pad and paper to the interview to take notes. Remember that you want to give the employer your full, undivided attention, so only take brief notes during the interview to jot down things you may not remember accurately, such as specific figures or names. Collect business cards from everyone you meet, if possible.

Immediately upon leaving the interview, stop in the lobby or in your car, and take notes. Do this as soon as possible because you will forget a large portion of information in just the time it takes to drive home.

Write down the key points of the meeting, personal information about your interviewer, and any other observations that may be helpful to you. Are you on a first name basis? Did you meet anyone else, and what were their names and titles? What was the assistant's name? What were the highlights of the meeting? How was your performance? Was there anything you forgot to bring up? What is the next step? When will they make a decision? Who is the real decision maker? Are there any other candidates? What was your impression of the company and your interviewer? What will help you get the job offer?

Use this information in your follow-up strategies.

# Send a Thank-You Letter
# After an Interview.

This letter is much more than a simple thank-you note. Just when the employer is sifting through her thoughts about the best candidate for the job, she receives a well-written letter from you. It is your last chance to sell yourself, reiterate your top qualifications, and express interest in the position. Fortunately for you, few job hunters take this step so it helps you stand out more, just like every other detail of your job search. Employers notice and appreciate consistent professionalism, organization, and attention to detail.

Write your letter the same day as your interview, and mail it within twenty-four hours. The sooner the employer receives it, the better for you. If the decision is being made within one or two days, hand deliver the letter the next morning. Faxing it or using e-mail is okay, but mailing it or hand delivering it makes a better impression.

This letter should be typed on stationery matching your resume, using a business style. Do not use handwritten notes. Begin your letter simply by thanking the employer for her time and mentioning the position. The second paragraph is used to bring up highlights of the meeting and mention your qualifications that the employer was most interested in. Answer the question, "Why should the employer hire me?" If you need two paragraphs, fine, but don't go over one page in length. The last paragraph is similar to the first, thanking her again, and stating your interest in the job.

If a second interview was scheduled, be sure to mention it.

# Research the Pay Range for Your Job Target.

Yes, you heard right. More research. Actually, you can research this portion at any time during your job search, but particularly before an interview. Why not skip the work and just go in like everyone else and aim for the top? How will you know what the top is? If you spend the time now to research pay ranges, it will pay off handsomely. Your research could easily reward you with an extra $3,000 to $4,000 in starting pay per year. If you work there four years, that's $12,000 to $16,000 (or more!). Not bad pay for a day or two of research.

First, figure out what is the minimum pay you would accept, taking into account your living expenses. Then add ten percent to that figure. That number is your bottom line.

What pay range can you reasonably expect for your target work? There are several ways to find out. You already know the pay scale if you are seeking the same type of work as your last job. Learn pay ranges from informational interviewing, networking with contacts, research at the library or on the internet, and other interviews. The most reliable way is through interviewing with other companies and networking with people who work in your target company or hold a similar position in another company. On the internet, look up salary surveys at http://jobsmart.org/tools/salary/index.html.

Estimate the company's or the position's pay range. Another way to determine a range is to know the salary of the person below you and above you. Once you are armed with the most accurate pay range for your target job, you're ready to negotiate.

## *Negotiate for Top Dollars.*

Can you answer the question, "What pay do you want?" How you answer this question could cost you the job, or cost you thousands of dollars per year for naming a figure too low, or *pay* you thousands of dollars per year.

The number one rule: don't talk about pay until a job offer has been tendered or *strong hiring interest* is shown. The employer must be sold on you, and must want you, before you start talking about pay. Why? Because once the employer is convinced that you are the perfect candidate for the position, that is the strongest platform from which to negotiate.

Remember three key points: 1) the employer normally has a pay range in mind, 2) salary is usually negotiable and, 3) the best time to get a raise is before you're hired!

Another rule of negotiation is that the person who names a figure first, loses. The employer may ask about your salary history. Try to answer without naming a specific figure (too high or too low can kick you out of the running anyway), then turn the question around. Examples:

"The pay at my last job was (within or above) industry standards, plus (bonuses, incentive pay, benefits, stock options, profit sharing, etc.) What sort of incentive plans do you have?"

"The responsibilities (or job description) of this position are different than my last job. I don't believe my past pay is relevant in this case. What pay range did you have in mind for this position?"

"I was paid well due to my performance. What kind of pay can a top performer expect in this position?"

Know the pay range for this position (see *Research the Pay Rrange for Your Job Target*, p. 199.) When the employer asks what pay you want, try to get them to name the figure first.

"Let me recap my understanding of the position..." Describe the scope of authority, responsibilities, and expectations of the job with special attention to how you fit the position. "Is that how you see it?" Once that is agreed on, ask the employer, "Do you think I'm the right person for the job? What figure did you have in mind for someone of my experience and skills?" or "What does your company believe this work is worth?"

The employer will name a low figure first. After all, his job is to get the best candidate for the lowest pay. Never accept the first figure, but don't turn it down or scoff at it, either. As long as it's in your range, or has room to escalate to your range, you're fine. Once the employer names a number, try these strategies to raise it:

"The salary is lower than I expected, but I'm very interested in the position. Is there any flexibility in that figure?" or "Could more be justified in view of (your best selling point)?"

"Is $____ within the budget?" or "I appreciate the offer, but I'll have to think about it. I was expecting more in the line of $___."

If you must name the figure, express it in a range such as low forties, to give you room to negotiate. After you name it, BE SILENT, no matter how long it takes. Observe the employer. Is he nonchalant? Shocked? Laughing? If he doesn't bat an eye, you're in the right range. Now convince him you should be paid at the top of your range. If he is shocked or laughing, you have to determine if the reaction is real. He might fake it to solicit a lower salary from you. Either way, hold your ground and ask "What did you have in mind?"

Now is the time to look at the benefit package. Review vacation times, raises and reviews, health insurance, stock options, training and education, your office, bonuses and other perks. Try adding more benefits to make up for a lower salary. As a last resort, offer to start at a lower pay with a review and salary raise in sixty or ninety days. **Warning:** Get any negotiated changes in benefits and salary in writing before you begin the new job or send the employer a letter outlining your agreements.

One last word on negotiating for top pay. Delay your final decision. If you have played your cards right, the employer wants you and must have you. Delaying your decision for at least twenty-four hours will cause the employer to think you're not satisfied with the salary or you are considering other offers. Chances are good that he will up the ante on the spot. Or in a couple of days, call the employer and say you have thought it over and you really want the position, but the pay is a little low. "Is it possible to go to $\_\_?" or "Can we possibly raise it any?"

Negotiating is an art. You have to rely on your own judgment. As you can see, having the experience of a couple of interviews and negotiations under your belt is beneficial. Of course, none of this works unless the employer is sold on you, and that's why you do everything else in this book.

# *Call the Employer After an Interview.*

The follow-up strategies after an employment interview keep your name in the employer's mind while she is making a decision and demonstrates your persistence and enthusiasm for the job. Of course, follow-up strategies also give *you* feedback on what's happening.

You have already written and mailed your after interview letter within twenty-four hours of your interview. Call the employer after a week has passed or earlier if they are making the decision sooner.

When you get the employer on the line, thank her for the interview, and briefly express your enthusiasm for the position and why you are the right person for the job. Here are a couple of lines to move the employer closer to a decision:

"Have you contacted my references? What was your opinion?"

"When will you make a decision?"

"When do you want the job filled?"

"I'm very interested in the position and know I can make a contribution to the company. What do you think?"

"When can I start?"

"I'm available to start immediately (or in ____ days or weeks). Does that fit in with your time frame?"

"What do I have to do to get the job?"

If you can't reach the employer by phone, talk to the assistant. Ask if he remembers you and state that you are interested in the position and would like to speak to the employer if possible. The assistant may tell you when the decision is being made. If he likes you, he may even reveal how many final candidates there are. Ask if you can leave an e-mail message or voice mail for the employer.

Stay in touch until the final decision is made, because situations can and do change, and you want to be ready to step in. The employer may postpone hiring for a while due to any number of reasons. She may fill the position from inside the company, leaving another position open (new job lead), or she may create an entirely new position. Even if the employer does fill the position, the candidate could turn it down at the last minute, or the candidate might not work out, and the job would open again.

# What Do You Do If You Are not Hired?

Will statistics help? On the average, one job offer is tendered for every five interviews. If you follow the principles in this book, you will improve your ratio of job offers to interviews. Sometimes, no matter how brilliant you are or how perfect you were for that job, it just doesn't happen. You may never know the real reason you weren't hired. Perhaps the candidate who got the job was the granddaughter of a good friend of the president. Or you remind the employer of her despised sister-in-law.

Once you have been informed that the position was filled, your goal is to try to get a referral from the employer. Call the interviewer and state you're sorry it didn't work out, but does she know of anyone else who may be able to use your talents? If you can't reach her by phone, try e-mail, voice mail, or a short letter. Ask the assistant for referrals. It's also possible the company may have other openings in the near future.

Do not bludgeon yourself with all the things you did wrong. If you focus on the negative, your brain locks on it and reminds you of those negative images every time you interview. Instead, focus on the positive. What did you do right? What can you do to improve the next interview?

Expect rejections but don't dwell on them. They are a fact of life. Then get on with your life and your job search. Remember that every "no" gets you closer to a "YES!"

# Chapter Seven

# Gold Medal Techniques

# Get Promoted.

Instead of leaving your company, how about moving up? Or moving laterally to another position that interests you? Your experience with the company is a valuable asset. Many companies cross-train employees, especially management, so they have a better understanding of how the various departments interlace, which contributes to better efficiency, increased production, and healthier profits.

Many people climb the corporate ladder by starting with an entry level position such as administrative assistant or technician and work their way up. If you are in a mid-level position and want to change careers, how about a different position within your company? You already know the industry, product, and company. You would just be learning a new function.

Ask yourself the following questions. What more can I be doing to contribute to the company? What other departments interest me? What other department could use my current skills and knowledge? What are the goals of the company and my department? How can I contribute more to these goals? If I could implement any change for improvement, what would it be? How can I make my job or department more efficient or productive?

Talk to your boss about the goals of your department and company if you don't already know them. Formulate what you can do to contribute to those goals. What changes would you make? What ideas do you have to save money, increase production or sales, or be more efficient? Talk to your boss about your ideas with an open mind. Ask her what she thinks and if she has any other suggestions.

If you want to completely change functions, talk to people in the department that interests you. Find out about the different jobs people do, how the department works, what the boss is like, and what the people are like. Formulate how you could contribute to the department—how you would fit in. Casually talk to the department head about your interest. Caution: The department head may talk to your boss and sometimes bosses do not like people transferring out of their department. If your boss is that way, wait until there is an opening before you approach the other department head, or speak to him in confidence if you trust him to honor it.

# *Do Volunteer Work.*

Doing volunteer work during your job search has a three-fold benefit: you will learn new skills or polish your current skills, make new contacts, and psychologically receive a lift from helping others.

Volunteer work is an excellent way to learn and hone new skills without the expense of taking a class. You're gaining real-life experience and abilities that you may use in a new job. Volunteer work should be on your resume and mentioned in interviews, as long as it's relevant to your job target. After all, it is experience whether you're paid or not. I've worked with many women who re-entered the job market successfully by emphasizing their often-considerable volunteer work and the skills they used for that work.

As you become involved in a non-profit organization, you will make friends and valuable contacts. Remember, your contacts don't have to be in the same field you are targeting—job leads can come from anyone. Obviously, if your volunteer work is connected to your job target, you will benefit, too. Some companies have favorite charities and causes. Find out what they are, and join up! It's an excellent way to make good contacts who are familiar with you and your work.

Psychologically, helping others keeps your mind off your own problems and frustrations. No matter how bad things are, there is always someone who can benefit from your help. Contributing to others well being can be an inspirational, rewarding experience.

# *Learn Public Speaking.*

Does the thought of interviewing give you cold feet? Does your job target require that you give presentations? Or speak to groups? If this has you petrified, relax. Fear of public speaking is the number one fear in America, beating out fear of death at number two.

Toastmasters is an international organization dedicated to teaching and practicing public speaking, with chapters in most communities. In my home town of Phoenix, Arizona, there are more than forty clubs, large and small.

You will learn the dynamics of all kinds of public speaking from prepared speeches to impromptu speeches, humorous to inspirational, selling to informational, and story telling to leading a group discussion. The club's format is designed to help even the most timid speaker learn and grow. An added benefit is that you will make lots of friends, too.

Years ago, after I started my job search firm, I attended a meeting for a large organization for unemployed professionals. The audience numbered 150. I wanted desperately to speak to this group, knowing I had a lot to offer the attendees. There was one huge obstacle—I was petrified to speak in public. I joined Toastmasters, and six months later I gave a thirty-minute presentation to the same group and it was well received. Then I developed a series of seminars for the group.

If you are like most people who fear public speaking and want to overcome your fear, or you want to improve your public speaking skills, join Toastmasters. Many members have reported that Toastmasters helped them tremendously during employment interviews and to improve presentations skills necessary for their work. Look in your local yellow pages under Associations for Toastmasters International or call their headquarters at 714-858-8255 for the location nearest you.

# Be an Independent Contractor or Work Part-Time

Sometimes your ideal job is not quite attainable right away. Or it may take longer than you anticipated to land the job. Meanwhile, the bills keep mounting, and it becomes necessary to bring in some money *now*.

Having a part-time job or doing work as an independent contractor can help fill the gap and allow you time to continue your job search. These two options also provide a way to try out a type of work before you commit wholeheartedly to it.

Part-time positions often are the only starting positions available in some businesses or organizations such as airlines, UPS, Federal Express, and the United States Post Office. If you can live with a part-time paycheck, it can work for you.

Often, people desire a part-time position so they can be home with their children when school lets out. More and more employers

217

are offering flex time, job sharing, and part-time work to attract good workers who desire non-traditional working hours.

An independent contractor is someone who performs specific work on a contractual basis, often to large corporations who outsource certain types of work. Small companies also outsource work. If you had to go out into the world tomorrow and sell your talents as an independent contractor, what would you be doing? Often an independent contractor's first customer is her last employer. You might pleasantly surprise yourself by lining up some good jobs then decide you want to be self-employed.

## *Start Your Own Business.*

This is a tricky one. It is so easy to get lured into the seduction of starting your own business. Just when your frustration levels with your company, boss, or being an employee are the highest, starting your own business looks very attractive. Self-employment offers the definite advantages of being your own boss, making your own decisions, cutting through the red tape, and doing things your way. Remember that you will always have a boss—your customer!

**Warning:** Starting a business is harder than finding a job.

You may think you can avoid the whole job hunting process by starting your own business. If you do, you will be looking for work *every day*, for as long as you have your business. Your pay will be a roller coaster ride, and you may not make anything for six months, a year, or longer, while at the same time pumping money into your business.

If you're convinced you want to try it, start with identifying your skills and knowledge (see *Name Your Top Five Skills*, p. 19) and your favorite industries. What kind of work can you do to use your skills in your favorite industry? Are people willing to pay outsiders for this type of work? How much do they pay? How will you find your customers? Why will people want *you* to perform this work? Where will you perform this work? How much overhead will you have? How much money do you need to make to meet your living expenses? Are you willing to wear many hats in order to be self-employed?

Creating a business plan is highly recommended. It forces you to describe your business realistically and put the numbers in place. Writing one is easy to do on your computer with business plan software. The plan will help you to make an informed, educated decision. Conduct informational interviews with other business owners.

❦ Marissa wanted to start a clothing boutique business. She interviewed three mall managers for rental figures. Other research was based on her previous retail experience, interviewing people in the business, information in books, and advice of the Small Business Bureau. In a business plan software program, she entered all the figures and was astounded at the start-up costs and how much she had to earn to break even. She chucked the idea of the clothing boutique. However, she did start another successful business, with far less risk.

# *Work as a Temp.*

Another alternative and successful job hunting tactic is to work for a temporary employment agency. These assignments can last from a few weeks to several months. A rapidly increasing number of companies use temps to fill their employment needs, from clerical to mid-level and high-level positions requiring advanced skill levels. Millions of temporary employees are college-educated professionals: engineers, lawyers, managers, consultants, accountants, computer programmers, teachers, physicians, and nurses.

Besides filling in a heavy work-load, many employers believe it's beneficial to "try out" temporary employees before they hire them. The hiring, training, and termination process can be very expensive, so hiring temps, as opposed to hiring employees, can sometimes save money for the company in the end. According to industry statistics, thirty-eight percent of temps have been offered full-time employment at companies where they were on assignment.

For the worker, temping has attractive benefits, too. Temporary employees can try out various jobs to see whether they like that particular work and try out companies. The temp can fill a variety of positions for a variety of companies. If you want to learn new skills, or gain experience in new field, temping is a good way to do it. Temping also allows you to make new contacts in your target field.

Temporary employment allows you to earn money, gain skills and experience, and explore various jobs and companies while you continue your job search. However, you may be working full-time and not be able to make job search phone calls during business hours. Never make calls from your temp job. Leave the premises at lunch or your break and use a pay phone or cell phone.

## *Plan B or Burn Your Boats?*

Plan B is to have an alternate job search plan ready to go in case your number one job target doesn't work out. Remember the saying, "Don't put all you eggs in one basket."? Plan B is to have alternative job targets, alternative target companies (not just one or two), and to use alternative job search methods.

On the other hand, the "burn your boats" concept is: If there is no retreat, no choice, you *must* succeed. The story from which this concept is derived tells of a general who attacks another country and arrives by sea. He realizes that they are greatly outnumbered. Upon landing on the shores of the enemy country, he orders his own ships to be burned to the ground. The soldiers, witnessing the destruction of their only escape route, know there is only one way out—victory! Against insurmountable odds, they win the battle.

Having Plan B makes sense in a logical way, but if you have spent all this time and trouble to identify your ideal work and your dream job, why should you try something else? The key here is how realistic you are. Are you truly qualified to do the work you're targeting? If not, are you aiming for a lower position, that you *are* qualified to perform, that will *lead* to your dream job? Are you aiming for more than one company, preferably at least five? Are you using a variety of successful job search methods? Are you spending forty hours per week, or twenty if employed, on your job search?

My motivational method: Aim for work you love, be flexible, and burn your boats.

# Hang With Successful People.

When I first wanted to be a writer, with no experience and a few classes under my belt, I joined a writer's association. At my first meeting, I was impressed and intimidated at the same time. At my table, I met writers who had published books, written articles for prestigious publications, and sold screenplays to Hollywood. I volunteered to be the newspaper editor to learn more about writing and rub elbows with successful writers. Working on the newsletter honed my writing skills—it was proofread by two officers, and for a writer's association, it had to be perfect. The contacts I made were invaluable, providing advice, encouragement, and knowledge. Jokingly, I told people, "I want to be a successful writer, so I thought I would hang around other successful writers and maybe it would rub off." It does rub off.

Are you hanging with successful people? Successful people have a passion and energy about them. Most successful people want to help others be successful—other people who are not looking for a handout, but have a positive outlook on life and are working to improve themselves and achieve their goals.

How do you meet successful people? Where are they? Look to your friends, relatives, acquaintances, and co-workers. Join organizations and volunteer your time for a worthy cause. Make it a point to maintain contact with successful people and the new ones you meet. When a friend or acquaintance experiences a success, large or small, send a card or flowers or call them with your congratulations. We all love to be recognized for our accomplishments.

Hang with successful people. It rubs off.

## *Keep Your Job.*

There is no job security. No one owes you a job. There is no company loyalty. These are the lessons learned from the eighties and early nineties. If you haven't learned it from first hand experience, then believe it now.

You are responsible for your own productivity and your own career path, no matter what type of work you do. The only true loyalty is loyalty to yourself. The better you are, the better you perform your work, the more in demand you are. Instead of working "for" a company, join your fellow workers and customers to improve productivity, products, and services, produce better results, and achieve common goals.

Follow these steps to keep your work interesting, challenging, and excellent.

1. Keep a journal of your accomplishments.

2. Inventory your skills every six months or annually.

3. Know the goals of your company and department.

4. Formulate how to contribute to the goals using your skills.

5. Share your ideas and plans with your manager, peers, and employees.

6. Carry out your plan. Be flexible, and make changes if necessary.

Learn new skills and gain knowledge by taking classes and seminars offered by your company, universities, and community colleges. Read trade journals, books, and magazines to keep abreast of new developments in your field. Join associations related to your work, become an officer or chair a committee.

Stay in touch with your network you have worked so hard to develop. Thank them for their help, and let them know what you are doing. Make it a point to have lunch once a week with an acquaintance you haven't seen for a while.

Make a commitment to excel in the work you love. Operate from passion instead of fear or indifference, and you will live and work with joy.

# Book Order Form

Quantity

**JobFinder: How to Find a Better Job Faster**
ISBN: 0-9653868-4-8, 164 pgs., $12.95
Want a rewarding, enriching job? Use this practical,
step-by-step guide to help you find your ideal job, pronto.
Includes selling your talents to prime employers, acing
the interview, and negotiating for top dollars!

**Job Search Secrets: Smart Strategies to Land
Your Dream Job**
ISBN: 0-9653868-8-0, 230 pgs., $11.95
One hundred top-notch secrets of successful job hunters.
A motivational and inspiring way to land your dream job.

Shipping: $3.50 + .50 for each additional book.
Add 7.2% sales tax for orders in Arizona
Pay by (circle one)   check   money order   credit card
MasterCard   Visa   American Express   Discover

Total amount--Make check payable to WorkLife Publishing

Mailing Address:          Credit card number:
WorkLife Publishing       _____
4532 E. Grandview Rd.     Exp. Date_____
Phoenix, AZ  85032        Signature _____

888-596-9675   602-493-9321 fax
Visit our web site: www.worklifepublishing.com

# About the Author

Claudia Jordan is a job search consultant, job coach, author and speaker who has helped thousands of job hunters land their dream jobs. As a speaker on job search topics, Ms. Jordan has been a talk show guest on national television and radio talk shows, and a seminar leader at colleges and various organizations. She is the author of two job search books, *JobFinder: How to Find a Better Job Faster,* and *Job Search Secrets: Smart Strategies to Land Your Dream Job.* The book *JobFinder* was adopted immediatly as a college text book.

Ms. Jordan founded a job search firm in 1989, coaching individual job hunters how to successfully market themselves to win their dream jobs. As a business manager in the retail trade for seven years, she gained early experience in interviewing, hiring and training. She currently resides in Phoenix, Arizona with her family.